THE PROPHETIC IMPERATIVE

THE PROPHETIC IMPERATIVE

Social Gospel in Theory and Practice

SECOND EDITION

Richard S. Gilbert

Skinner House Books
Boston

Printed in Canada

Cover design by Suzanne Morgan

Photo by Nancy Pierce

ISBN 1-55896-411-8
978-1-55896-411-2

Library of Congress Cataloging-in-Publication Data

Gilbert, Richard S., 1936–
    The prophetic imperative : social gospel in theory and practice / Richard S. Gilbert.
        p. cm.
    Includes bibliographical references (p.) and index.
    ISBN 1-55896-411-8 (alk. paper)
        1. Church and social problems—Unitarian Universalist Association.   2. Unitarian Universalist Association—Doctrines.   I. Title.

BX9856.G55 2000
261.8–dc21

                                                                                00-063763

10 9 8 7 6 5 4 3
08 07 06

A study guide is available at www.uua.org/re/curriculum

Contents

Contents

Foreword

If you care about the future of progressive religion, if you seek to revive its impact on society, then you have opened the right book. The faith expounded here is humanistic, inclusive, and prophetic. Richard Gilbert is no mere theoretician. He is, and has been throughout an exemplary ministry of nearly forty years, a practitioner of the faith he advocates: publicly engaged religious leadership, seeking to help create what Dr. King called "the Beloved Community" for us all.

Modernity has come to regard religion as "a private matter." The better side of this transformation is that religious values, convictions, affiliations, and beliefs have come to be seen as subject to personal reflection and choice. The more dangerous side is represented by the infection of religion itself with the self-involved, narcissistic spirit of a prosperous society. When "spirituality" is only about the inner life and does not involve concern for others—especially for the most vulnerable among us—then there is a need to ask if this is truly an authentic form of religious living.

Unitarian Universalism, as Richard Gilbert well knows, feels perhaps uniquely called to support a progressive, prophetic conception of public ministry and the public church. The "public church," of whatever tradition, according to American historian of religion Martin Marty, is the religious community that is not content simply to serve the spiritual needs of the gathered congregation. It feels called to serve and to address the wider community as well; to challenge social evil and to help heal its social wounds. Our congregations may not have creeds, out of respect for individual conscience in matters of faith, but they have always had a strong sense of covenantal calling to serve the whole community, and to do so in the spirit of the prophets of all ages and places.

As President of the Unitarian Universalist Association, I sense this calling every day. Situated on Boston's Beacon Street, next door to the State House and across from the Boston Common, our headquarters and my office are placed clearly on the public square. This reflects the heritage of our oldest and most historic churches in the towns of Eastern Massachusetts—on the town common, at the heart of civic life. When I receive visitors in my office—especially youth groups—I often ask them to take note of the portrait of Susan B. Anthony in my office. She was a member of the congregation that Richard Gilbert now serves. Though her life ended before her crusade for women's rights saw the passage of the Nineteenth Amendment to the Constitution, she exemplified the prophetic spirit. Her determination was not only to develop and to express her own spiritual, moral, intellectual, and organizational power as a woman, but to help make sure that others would have the opportunity to help shape history, rather than just being pushed around by it.

Then I point out the window to the statue of Horace Mann on the State House lawn. That Unitarian layman gave up his position as president of the state senate to give his life to the cause of free public education for all. Across the street is the monument to young Unitarian abolitionist Robert Gould Shaw and the members of Fifty-fourth Regiment of Massachusetts Volunteers—the band of freed slaves who, with Shaw as their colonel, gave their lives in the struggle against slavery.

I challenge my visitors, especially the younger ones, to learn more about the lives and history of these prophetic figures and people like them. The age of prophetic living must not stay imprisoned in the past; it must be revived in every generation as our own. As one of our hymns puts it, "Revelation is not sealed./ Answ'ring now to our endeavor,/ truth and right are still revealed."

Only in a romantic conception of the prophets, however, do these revelations come to isolated individuals. Most authentic inspiration really comes through and in community life. Richard Gilbert knows that. He begins by relating the historical background to the social justice commitment of his own religious people and analyzing social justice's current role (or lack thereof) in our congregations. In the second half of the book, he provides practical advice for congregations on mobilizing all of their members and doing the work effectively. He offers the benefits of a lifetime of experience shaping a community capable of inspiring and serving not only the individuals within, but also the community and the world beyond its walls.

Richard Gilbert aspires, in the tradition of James Luther Adams, to encourage "the prophethood of *all* believers." In these pages he puts a choice before us all: the continued privatization of our religious lives—or the potential revival of prophetic, socially engaged religious living.

In many ways it is a choice between death and life—for fully faithful religious living, for fully faithful religious communities, and for a spiritually sound and just society.

Richard Gilbert was ordained to the Unitarian Universalist ministry in 1961—the year that the Unitarian and Universalist movements in North America formed a new association. He began as an urban minister in Cleveland, then served a campus community in Ithaca, New York, and since 1970 has been parish minister of the First Unitarian Church of Rochester, New York, in a congregation and association long committed to its public ministry.

In an earlier edition, Richard Gilbert's commitment to "the prophetic imperative" has already inspired many religious leaders, including this one. Here he offers even more. Revive your own commitment to making faithful choices. Remember that this truly *is* the religious imperative of our time.

John A. Buehrens, President
Unitarian Universalist Association
of Congregations
August 2000

Preface

Since the first edition of *The Prophetic Imperative* was published in 1980, theological discourse has changed dramatically. Liberation theology in all its modes—feminist, African, African American, Latino, Asian—has seriously challenged traditional theological categories. When I did my doctoral work, upon which this book is based, in the late seventies, we had moved from the activist sixties, when I had cut my teeth on religious social responsibility, to the navel-gazing seventies, when ego reigned. The book was to be a rallying cry to action. The political climate then moved from the seventies through the "greed is good" eighties to the militantly conservative, privatized nineties. The shape of justice in the new millennium is uncertain.

The mainline churches have been marginalized and face a confident fundamentalist political theology. Liberal religion, in its Unitarian Universalist expression, has not been immune to any of these currents. Consequently, it is a good time for a reassessment. What are the religious foundations for social justice work among Unitarian Universalist congregations, and what is our mission among the community of faiths in the public arena as we move into the new millennium?

A brief autobiographical note will provide the reader with the particular perspective and the inevitable biases from which I write. When I was working on a doctorate in Ethics and Society at the University of Chicago Divinity School in 1964–1965, I became increasingly frustrated with my academic burdens. I had planned to pursue a course of study that would prepare me for an effective social ministry. But the emphasis there was academic: The school's mission was based more on educating researchers and teachers of religion than on teaching ministers to be more effective social change agents.

The murder of Unitarian Universalist minister James Reeb impelled me to make an urgent trip to Selma, Alabama; I was once again immersed, in the words of Justice Oliver Wendell Homes, in the "actions and passions of the time." My experience in Brown's Chapel, where I heard Martin Luther King, Jr.'s eulogy, was the most riveting religious experience of my adult life. When I returned, I knew the practical would always have ascendancy over the academic in my life and career. I left Chicago for a five-year ministry in Ithaca, New York, where I was thrust into anti-Vietnam War activism with Father Daniel Berrigan and into the racial turmoil on campus. Doctoral work at Chicago seemed very far away, yet I still longed to bring some discipline to my social philosophy and that of the liberal church.

When I was called by the First Unitarian Church of Rochester, New York, these two inclinations—the practical and the theoretical— at last came together. Here I was minister of a large urban church with a reputation for being Rochester's hospitable roof and alert conscience. It was a perfect living laboratory. Not far from where I live is Colgate Rochester Divinity School, where Social Gospel pioneer Walter Rauschenbusch taught. It was a good combination. From 1974 to 1977 I moved, sometimes easily, sometimes uneasily, between minister-in-community and scholar-in-residence. I continued my ministry at the First Unitarian Church while taking one course per term at CRDS, filling summers with research and writing.

The Doctor of Ministry program at the school was designed to integrate active ministry with academic reflection. So intimate was the connection that, from time to time, my faculty advisor noted that some of my papers sounded suspiciously like sermons. He was not far off the mark. At Chicago, I knew what I wanted to do: develop the foundations for a new Social Gospel by exploring the possibilities for justice making. I did not want to detach myself from my culture with a theological tome that might earn a degree but collect dust on a shelf— of interest only to scholars or seminary students in need of reference material. I wanted to produce an academically respectable but pragmatic guide for the liberal church as it struggled with its mission in society.

This is not a how-to-save-the-world book, but a challenge to mind and conscience in the context of a church community. We have perhaps learned that true self-actualization, salvation, and fulfillment have to do with both personal meaning and social responsibility. The two do not compete; they reinforce one another. By the same token, our churches have matured. We are in the process of learning that church social action is not a small band of marginal activists in the church decrying church inaction or seeking to represent the whole church. Rather, it is a congregational process of coming to terms with the mission of the religious community in a society that sometimes confuses the separation of church and state with the divorce of religion and public policy.

This is a good place to be—within the continuing tension of piety and prophecy, spirituality and society, individual and community. It is through this tension that we will work out our common destiny. I am gratified that *The Prophetic Imperative* has been useful to a number of individuals and congregations as they engage in the arduous task of discerning what Unitarian Universalists have to contribute to the world. As we face a very "unbrave" new world, it is imperative that Unitarian Universalists take seriously the prophetic tradition that has been so central to our history and faith.

THEORETICAL FOUNDATIONS

CHAPTER ONE

Living under
the Prophetic Imperative

In the year that King Uzziah died I saw the Lord sitting down
upon a throne, high and lifted up; and his train filled the temple. Above him stood the seraphim; each had six wings: with
two he covered his face, and with two he covered his feet, and
with two he flew. And one called to another and said: "Holy,
holy, holy is the Lord of hosts and the whole world is full of
his glory." And the foundations of the thresholds shook at the
voice of him who called, and the house was full of smoke. And
I said: "Woe is me! For I am lost; for I am a man of unclean lips,
and I dwell in the midst of a people of unclean lips; for my
eyes have seen the King, the Lord of hosts!" Then flew one of
the seraphim to me, having in his hand a burning coal which
he had taken with tongs from the altar. And he touched my
mouth, and said: "Behold, this has touched your lips; your
guilt is taken away, and your sin forgiven." And I heard the
voice of the Lord saying, "Whom shall I send, and who will go
for us?" Then I said, "Here I am! Send me."

—*Isaiah 6:6–8*

A placard on a bulletin board at the University of Rochester a few
years ago invited students to take part in a two-day research project on
empathy training. But someone had crossed out the first two letters of
"empathy" and put an "a" over them. What is not required in our time
is "apathy training," for the American people are already well
schooled in that after the navel-gazing seventies, the greedy eighties,
and the sharp right turn of the reactionary nineties. Here, at the cusp
of the millennium, it is time once more to take our spiritual and moral
bearings.

Mary Berry of the U.S. Civil Rights Commission wrote in the July 15, 1985, issue of *U.S. News and World Report:* "We've been living on the gas-tank fumes of the protests of the 1960s—and the gas tank is empty. We've got to do it all over again." The point is as well taken now as it was then. New energy is required if we are not to abdicate responsibility for the state of the world to the more-than-eager Religious Right. Unitarian Universalists have historically struggled to "speak truth to power" in their own times. Thus, we were in the forefront of the Civil Rights and peace movements of the sixties and early seventies. Then our zeal seemed to flag in the narcissism of the seventies; we became victims of what the late Unitarian Universalist scholar and activist James Luther Adams called, in his 1977 Meadville/Lombard lectures, "the demonic of privatization." As a movement we were preoccupied with a kind of "self-actualization" that had more to do with personal growth of a psychological kind than with spiritual growth of a prophetic kind. With the neoconservative onslaught of the eighties, we were at first stunned, then angered, and then prompted to reassert what I call the "prophetic imperative." The militantly conservative nineties have been too much with us, and we need more than ever to assert our justice-making capacity before we are swept aside by such groups as the Christian Coalition, Focus on the Family, the Family Life Research Council, and their allies on the reactionary political and Religious Right.

When every day seems the anniversary of something awful, we do well to remember the story of the great-hearted soul who ran through the city streets crying, "Power, greed, and corruption. Power, greed, and corruption." For a time, the attention of the people was riveted on this single-minded, open-hearted person for whom all of life had become focused in one great question. But then everyone went back to work, only slightly hearing, some annoyed. Finally, a child stepped in front of the wailing figure on a cold and stormy night. "Elder," said the child, "don't you realize no one is listening to you?" "Of course I do," the elder answered. "Then why do you shout?" the child insisted, incredulous. "If nothing is changing, your efforts are useless." "Ah, dear child, I do not shout only in order to change them. I shout so that they cannot change me."

LIVING UNDER THE PROPHETIC IMPERATIVE

I contend that the Unitarian Universalist movement lives under a prophetic imperative, a religious mandate for the corporate address of the church to the systemic problems of society. I cannot prove that; I do not assert it as a divine imperative; I only feel it deep in my bones. Otherwise, we will be trapped in individualistic self-interest promoted by the dominant reactionary rhetoric and by neoconservative ideology, both political and religious.

George Bernard Shaw once suggested that every citizen of a civilized society ought to be brought before the bar of justice periodically to justify their existence. If they could not do so, they should summarily be put to death. While this is a bit of Shavian hyperbole, it merits the serious reflection of spiritually alive people.

I think of the Reverend Henry Meserve's provocative question: "If you were arrested for being a Unitarian Universalist, would there be enough evidence to convict you?" Clearly, a number of our forebears would have been convicted. We know the stories of Benjamin Rush and Thomas Jefferson, William Ellery Channing and Theodore Parker, Hosea and Adin Ballou, Thomas Starr King and Susan B. Anthony, Dorothea Dix and Clara Barton, Jane Addams, and John Haynes Holmes. Let us now praise these famous women and men, but let us not forget those common people of our heritage who have no memorial, who perished as though they had never been, people whose passion unfroze a rational religion and fired it with justice. They lived out the social gospel of their times. I believe that the foundations of a new social gospel are already available in the history, theology, ethics, and sociology that inform our movement.

PROPHETIC RELIGION

The term *prophetic* here refers to the scriptural tradition of ethical monotheism articulated in the Hebrew prophets, Micah, Amos, Isaiah, and others, with their emphasis on social justice. According to this tradition a prophet is a divinely inspired preacher. Prophecy in the Bible does not concern itself primarily with *fore*telling future events. It deals rather with *forth*telling the intuitively felt will of God for a specific situation in the life of an individual or nation. Prophets were those to whom God revealed divine secrets. God "whispered in their pearly ears," to quote my seminary Bible professor, Morton Scott Enslin. These prophets pointed out the perils of wickedness, confidently proclaiming what the people ought to do to realize the Kingdom of God, an ideal social order. James Luther Adams, himself one of the prophetic figures in twentieth-century Unitarian Universalism, pointed out in *The Prophethood of All Believers* that the acceptable understanding of prophet when doctoral candidates faced their feared dissertation interrogation was "The prophet was one who proclaimed doom!" By this he meant that the prophet predicted disaster when the nation Israel did not follow the divine commands.

In his 1977 lectures at the Meadville/Lombard Theological School mid-winter conference Adams told of a long conversation he had with psychologist Erich Fromm on the broad questions of American culture. Because of Fromm's psychological orientation, Adams expected him to concentrate on inner space. Adams describes the conversation at one point as follows: "'Erich, what makes you tick?' To my surprise he replied: 'I think I know the answer to that question. It is Old Testament Messianism. The prophets believed that the meaning of life is the struggle for justice in community.'"

Thus the prophet Micah: "He has showed you, O man, what is good; and what does the Lord require of you but to do justice, and to love kindness, and to walk humbly with your God?" (6:8). Amos rails against temple ceremonies, which have eclipsed ethical religion: "I hate, I despise your feasts, and I take no delight in your solemn assemblies. . . . But let justice roll down like waters, and righteousness like an everflowing stream." (5:21, 24). Isaiah, in words that have formed the structure of Christian worship for centuries, takes up the challenge of ethical monotheism with the ringing declaration, "Here I am! Send me!" (6:8).

These prophets took time seriously. God was not only Creator of the natural world but also the Lord of history. They viewed human history in linear terms, not cyclical as in many Eastern religions. People were not creatures to be pushed around by history, but creatures who could respond to it by helping to shape it. The prophets were not so much predictors of the future as they were its architects. They dropped an ethical plumbline over Israel and found her wanting. They saw their mission as serving people by dealing with the structures of society that oppressed them.

The term *prophet* has traditionally referred to an individual. There were the prophets of ancient Israel, a group of individuals living in the eighth through the sixth centuries BCE. There are prophets of the human spirit, the founders of the great world religions and other pinnacle figures who shook the foundations of their time and ours. In a mass society with a bureaucratized ethos, it is much more difficult to think of individual prophets. To be sure, there are the individuals who tower over their times—Martin Luther King, Jr., Mahatma Gandhi, Albert Schweitzer, Jane Addams, Susan B. Anthony, and Rachel Carson. However, social change today requires much more than charismatic individuals. It requires the mobilization of individual energies into communal power.

My intent is to apply the term *prophetic* primarily to the religious community. The prophetic church is a religious community that seeks to intervene in human history for the sake of social justice. This intervention is made in the context of religious conviction, but without the supernatural confidence of the Hebrew prophets. This is rather a tall spiritual order. The authority of the prophetic liberal church will instead be derived in somewhat more humanistic terms that articulate a transcendent standard for justice.

The imperative to be stressed here is that which emerges from the disciplines of freedom. Freedom is not merely the absence of restraint, but the will and capacity to act on one's environment. It is a freedom that implies responsibility to enrich and expand freedom in the social order. Freedom, a central value of Unitarian Universalism, is a social concept, and if it is to be preserved, an obligation is placed on the free person. I believe we are not free to desist from struggling for freedom for self and others. Freedom, by its very nature, places an imperative claim on the free person to expand that freedom to all.

In the present context *imperative* has to do with a compulsion of conscience, personal and corporate, a sense of urgency to live out the ethical implications of religious faith. Such a religious mandate has sources inherent in the very nature of the liberal religious community, rather than an externally transcendent source, although the latter may be decisive for some among us.

Social Gospel refers to that historic turn-of-the-century movement in the American churches that sought to relate the church as a corporate entity to social problems. *Justice making* is one contemporary synonym for Social Gospel. The new social gospel I espouse is in historical continuity with the traditional social gospel, but it is sharply chastened by historical experience. The new gospel tempers an overly optimistic assessment of human nature and human institutions and the possibility of changing them. It recognizes the finite freedom that characterizes human nature and the persistence of self-interest inherent in human organizations. It will more fully recognize the stubbornness of the demonic forces of the social order and the institutional nature of social evil. It will see social responsibility as intrinsically related to the religious quest; it will not err in making the social gospel the whole gospel. It will not envision the Beloved Community as a goal realizable in any one period of history, but as a human ideal transcendent to human history. It will find historical meaning in struggling toward the Beloved Community in history. At the same time, it will value the basic insights of the old social gospel in discerning the role of the religious community in social change. It will appreciate the urgent commitments that are made by people and religious communities. It will define the church, among other things, as a social change agent and a transformer of culture. The focus will be on the Unitarian Universalist movement of the United States. While particular attention will be paid to the local congregation (especially in the latter part of the book), reference is also made to the movement as a whole.

I am advocating a corporate address to social problems, an institutional response rather than a merely individualistic one. The church is a social institution alongside other social groupings. It is appropriate for the religious community to self-consciously analyze its role in the society as an agency of potential power, a task difficult for the free church tradition with its stress on individualism.

SYSTEMIC SOCIAL CHANGE

Systemic change suggests that social action should be directed at underlying causes of social problems rather than merely at their symptoms. Treating symptoms alone, while often necessary, might well be a soporific to cover fundamental injustice, putting the proverbial Band-Aid on a cancer. Thus, food kitchens, however laudable, might merely feed the victims of a fundamentally unjust social order instead of rooting out the causes of their hunger. A systemic approach challenges the underlying premises of the American economy, which produces poverty in the midst of plenty and deals with public policy issues: taxation, government welfare programs, and income distribution, among others.

Systemic change contrasts with attitudinal change as the most effective way to achieve social justice. In the latter it is assumed that change is effected by working on individual attitudes before behavior can be modified ("You can't legislate morality!"). This is what I call the Billy Graham philosophy, according to which social change consists of bringing people to Christ; social amelioration automatically follows. In liberal circles, it is sometimes assumed this transformation comes through "consciousness raising," as if awareness of problems somehow inexorably leads to their solution.

Analysis of systemic change points to the frequent futility of this approach, showing that social injustice is caused more by irresponsible groups than guilty individuals. This was Reinhold Niebuhr's insight when he wrote of "moral man and immoral society." For example, despite all the preachments, civil rights progress for black people in this country came only when structures were changed by force of law. The *Brown v. Board of Education* decision of the Supreme Court in 1954 has come to be generally accepted as the beginning of the Civil Rights revolution. It is generally conceded that civil rights legislation was required to bring African Americans into the mainstream of American society. Social scientists point out that one of the most effective ways to change behavior is to alter the social structures in which people find themselves. The Marxist analysis of history likewise focuses on the need for structural change. Martin Luther King, Jr., reminded us that, while legislation cannot change the heart, it can restrain the heartless. Systemic change is built on these insights.

Editor Clifton Fadiman relates a story in *The Little, Brown Book of Anecdotes* about the legendary Republican Mayor Fiorello La Guardia of New York (1933–1945) that illustrates the nature of systemic change contrasted with charity. The mayor was presiding at the police court:

> One bitter cold day they brought a trembling old man before him, charged with stealing a loaf of bread. His family, he said, was starving. "I've got to punish you," declared La Guardia. "The law makes no exception. I can do nothing but sentence you to a fine of ten dollars." But the Little Flower was reaching into his pocket as he added, "Well, here's the ten dollars to pay your fine. And now I remit the fine." He tossed a ten-dollar bill into his famous sombrero. "Furthermore," he declared, "I'm going to fine everybody in this courtroom fifty cents for living in a town where a man has to steal bread in order to eat. Mr. Bailiff, collect the fines and give them to this defendant!" The hat was passed and an incredulous old man, with a light of heaven in his eyes, left the courtroom with a stake of forty-seven dollars and fifty cents.

SOCIAL RESPONSIBILITY: A TYPOLOGY

To provide a framework for considering social responsibility, I have chosen the typology *The Four Types of Social Concern* as developed by Thomas E. Price in a 1973 issue of *engage/social action* and later reprinted by the UUA. He suggests four basic options in describing the role of the church in society: social service, social education, social witness, and social action. Price stresses that these options are not mutually exclusive, but help clarify the relationship of institutional religion to social life.

Social service might well be thought of as the charitable approach, a direct rendering of service to those in need. It is good to reach out our hands in one-to-one contact with the neighbors whom we can see. The

Good Samaritan stopped by the side of the road to give direct assistance to the ravaged traveler. This is the most frequent expression of social responsibility. We are all familiar with relief efforts in time of disaster, Christmas baskets for the poor, and a personal ministry to those in prison, to cite but a few examples. At its best, however, social service is not merely charity—Lady Bountiful stretching out a gloved hand to give a crust of bread to a street urchin. When service is sensitively rendered, there is more going on than charity. When middle-class suburbanites spend time in the inner city, for example, they enter a world previously experienced only vicariously—in TV documentaries or novels like *Les Miserables,* curiously made into a popular Broadway musical. If done well, a real empathy with those presumed to be society's losers can develop. Those who take service seriously also begin to raise questions: Why, in this land of plenty and opportunity, are there people who do not know where their next meal is coming from or where they will spend the night?

This leads to a second dimension of social action, *social education.* It is not enough to bind up the wounds of the distressed traveler on the road to Jericho and leave some money for his care; it is important that we begin to understand what happened and why. What are the social and moral conditions that create poverty in the midst of plenty? Here we must enter the lists of sociology with its study of human behavior. We also examine economic forces, like the market, with its apparently inevitable division of persons into winners and losers. Political factors weigh heavily here as well, such as the general absence of the poor from the voting booth. The middle and upper classes essentially elect our leaders. Many of the poor, we learn, simply feel they have no stake in American society. Why bother?

Education can, of course, be dangerous. The consciousness-raising work of Paulo Freire as spelled out in *The Pedagogy of the Oppressed* enabled Brazilian peasants to read about their oppressed situation, which was the first step toward their radicalization and action. Education becomes a tool for social change. When we deepen our understanding of social problems, we may uncover the corruptions of power, greed, and irresponsibility. When we see the minimum wage lagging far behind the cost of living, we know there are powers that find it against their self-interest. We discover that the poor pay a disproportionate part of their earnings in taxes, even as middle-class people moan and take as a matter of right their tax write-offs on houses and other entitlements. Real social education, radical education, digs to the roots of our problems and reveals pictures that are often unpleasant for those in power to view.

Social education, seriously done, is the process by which persons learn about social issues in the light of a religious tradition. Again taking the Good Samaritan parable, we might expect to learn about the history of the road, the social background of the perpetrators of the crime, the alternatives for remedying the situation, and the religious motivation for doing something about it. Social education on public issues involves both a discussion of their content and an interpretation of this content in the context of ethical principles. Study and reflection are the components of this mode of social concern. Study groups, sermons, and documents for congregational study such as the Unitarian Universalist Association General Assembly Resolutions are illustrations.

When injustice is so exposed, another dimension of social responsibility becomes possible, *social witness*. This is the process of making public by word and/or deed the convictions of an individual or group on specific social issues. Social values are made public for the sake of making them public. They are brought to the public square in the pattern of the rhetoric of the Hebrew prophets who spoke "truth to power" by dropping the plumbline of justice over the injustice they observed and detested.

Many religious groups have a process of resolutions on matters of public concern by which they speak out on the issues of the day. Such statements are often credited with playing a key role in creating a climate conducive to the success of the civil rights movement, hastening the end of the Vietnam War, and challenging United States policy in Central America. Although cynics say such resolutions are no more efficacious than petitionary prayers (in which the supplicant urges God to intervene), it remains true that there is what Paul Tillich calls a "silent interpenetration" and shaping of the culture through the voice of religion. In the Good Samaritan scenario we might think of a silent vigil both to identify with the victim and to point out the danger on the road. Resolutions, fasts, sermons, street theater, marches, and picketing are all acts of social witness calling attention to an injustice. Witness is advocacy, but as long as it is isolated and not part of an organized effort to bring about social change, it remains witness.

Social action is distinguished from the other modes of social concern in that, as Price says, "(1) It is organized (implying group support for the objectives); (2) it attempts to influence policy makers and decision makers (implying a focus on structures rather than people)." Social action involves concentration on the causes rather than the symptoms of injustice—going beyond the Band-Aid. In the first century of the common era, this might have involved working to improve the lot of people whose impoverishment might lead them to crime—creating jobs by rebuilding the highway using previously unemployed laborers. This particular option comes closest to what has been called in this study "the prophetic imperative."

These four types of social responsibility are useful tools for social and moral analysis. Some years ago during the Reagan administration, at a meeting of Rochester's Southeast Ecumenical Ministry (SEM) clergy, the coordinator of our food cupboard read a directive from the U.S. Department of Health and Human Services. Henceforth, all private gifts of food and the like to indigent individuals would have to be reported and deducted from their federal benefits. Thus, people who ran out of food stamps at the end of the month and used the food cupboard to survive could never keep up, much less get ahead. What the right hand of charity gave out, the left hand of government would take away.

Many of us thought that food cupboards, food kitchens, and shelters were temporary expedients until the rising tide of the economy lifted all boats or until government took seriously its responsibility for the general welfare. What was happening before our very eyes was the privatization of welfare, a serious institutional expression of President Reagan's naive comment that the churches should take it over themselves. We were appalled at this governmental mandate. The harder we worked in the private sector, the harder the government worked at reducing people to total dependency. Evidently, many felt as we did, for there was such a storm of protest that the ruling was rescinded. The food cupboards, food kitchens, and shelters still cannot keep up with the demand, and never will so long as the systemic causes of this appalling poverty in the midst of plenty are not addressed. Welfare reform as promulgated in the 1996 Personal Responsibility Act seems to have carried out that view to its logical, or illogical, conclusion.

The SEM churches were at first dealing in direct service, a course of action with nearly unanimous support. A modest bit of social education told us that the federal government was exploiting not only service providers, who had to work harder and could not make headway, but also the needy people, many of them elderly and handicapped, who could never get beyond bare subsistence. Our social witness was to cry foul and mobilize our constituencies to speak out at this policy obscenity. Social action was to focus all this energy on the people in power and the policies they implement—with sermons, letter writing campaigns, and congressional visits. Policy reversal was the result.

Going after the Department of Health and Human Services is considerably more controversial than supporting a food cupboard or staffing a soup kitchen. Yet that is what will be required if any semblance of justice is to be realized in our land. It is so much easier to give someone bread to eat than to change the structures that make them hungry in the first place. I have never understood why the dependency created by charity is any better than dependency created by governmental programs.

The inadequacy of the market mechanism for millions; the issue of guaranteed economic rights to food and shelter, education, jobs and medical care; the tragedy of companies leaving communities with impunity while workers lose jobs; and union busting and right-to-work laws are rather controversial issues, yet they are at the heart of our quest for justice. To inveigh against poverty and to collect food for charitable distribution are laudable as far as they go, but they don't go far enough toward addressing the basic causes of social problems.

The Good Samaritan's ethical responsibility is not over after the traveler is healed and fed. What will become of the victim after this service? Will it happen again? Can the injured traveler find a job? Can the road be made safe for travel? Should someone seek out the reasons there are those up in the hills who descend to rob travelers? Do some people prefer doing evil to doing good? The parable of the Good Samaritan is far deeper in meaning than its casual and frequent Sunday morning reading would indicate.

If liberal churches can mobilize themselves only to create more and better food kitchens and do not resolutely seek out the causes of hunger in a land of plenty, if they build bigger and better shelters and do not challenge government's decimation of programs for housing the poor, if they fill yet more Thanksgiving and Christmas baskets and do not wonder what happens to people who must eat the whole year, then I charge they are ethically irresponsible.

Congregations must, of course, comfort the afflicted—not only their own members, not only the neighbors whom they can see in the soup kitchens and the shelters, but also the neighbors they cannot see across this nation and around this world who are caught up in decisions made by the powerful. There is a kernel of wisdom in the cynic's Golden Rule: those who have the gold make the rules. Responsible congregations will realize that too often such comforting, standing alone, may only serve to cover up injustice.

The apostle Paul wrote about the responsibility of Christians to confront principalities and powers as they sought to spread the gospel. Confronting the powers that be in our society—political, social, economic, and religious—can be unpleasant business. We, ourselves, may well be enmeshed in those powers. But if we fail to do so, we neglect the tradition of the Hebrew prophets who called a spade a spade, who named names, and who were ill content to demand justice in abstract terms that would endear them to all people. Jesus, in the tradition of the prophets, was a mover and a shaker who upset the power elite of his time with his challenge to wealth and privilege. I believe Unitarian Universalists live under a prophetic imperative to act in love for justice, the "priesthood of all believers" (Martin Luther) supplemented with the "prophethood of all believers" (James Luther Adams). We need to be equally skilled in comforting the afflicted and afflicting the comfortable, who, after all, may be us.

The "Parable of Good Works" in a social action primer *Must We Choose Sides?*, published by the Interreligious Task Force for Social Analysis, updates the parable of the Good Samaritan and dramatizes the potential conflict between these types of social concern.

Once upon a time there was a small village on the edge of a river. The people there were good and the life in the village was good. One day a villager noticed a baby floating down the river. The villager quickly jumped into the river and swam out to save the baby from drowning.

The next day this same villager was walking along the river bank and noticed two babies in the river. He called for help, and both babies were rescued from the swift waters. And the following day four babies were seen caught in the turbulent current. And then eight, then more, and still more.

The villagers organized themselves quickly, setting up watch towers and training teams of swimmers who could resist the swift waters and rescue babies. Rescue squads were soon working twenty-four hours a day. And each day the number of helpless babies floating down the river increased.

The villagers organized themselves efficiently. The rescue squads were now snatching many children each day. Groups were trained to give mouth-to-mouth resuscitation. Others prepared formula and provided clothing for the chilled babies. Many . . . were involved in making clothing and knitting blankets. Still others provided foster homes and placement.

While not all the babies, now very numerous, could be saved, the villagers felt they were doing well to save as many as they could each day. Indeed, the village priest blessed them in their good work. And life in the village continued on that basis.

One day, however, someone raised the question, "But where are all these babies coming from? Who is throwing them into the river? Why? Let's organize a team to go upstream and see who's doing it." The seeming logic of the elders countered: "And if we go upstream, who will operate the rescue operations? We need every concerned person here."

"But don't you see," cried the one lone voice, "if we find out who is throwing them in, we can stop the problem and no babies will drown. By going upstream we can eliminate the cause of the problem."

"It is too risky." And so the numbers of babies in the river increased daily. Those saved increased, but those who drowned increased even more.

COMPASSION FATIGUE

Many of us experience *compassion fatigue* in working toward the Beloved Community, but find our patience strengthened by the sardonic humor of I. F. Stone in his acerbic *I. F. Stone Weekly:* "Why, you can go weeks without seeing any change." And remember the unknown wit who wrote, "Most of the world's useful work is done by people who are pressed for time, or are tired or don't feel well."

I have also come to realize that, while the political positions we take are the result of reason, these experiences are full of convictions and passions. The experiences are transforming because people feel deeply and are committed to put their lives on the line. It is spiritually exhilarating to realize that in our small efforts, we are part of a great living stream of reformers, a great cloud of witnesses who seek to create the Beloved Community on Earth, who seek to place the stubborn ounces of our weight on the side of justice.

Our role cannot be better expressed than by Unitarian Universalist minister and author Robert Fulghum in *It Was on Fire When I Lay Down on It:* "I do not want your sympathy for the needs of humanity. I want your muscle. I do not want to talk about what you understand about this world. I want to know what you will do about it. I do not want to know what you hope. I want to know what you will work for."

DISCERNING THE SPIRIT OF THE TIMES

If we would redeem the times, then we must first discern them, as the apostle Paul suggested (Ephesians 5:16, Colossians 4:5). What is the zeitgeist, the characteristic spirit of our age? One dimension of that spirit is captured in a wartime story. It was standard procedure in wartime to have a runner who moves among the platoons gathering intelligence. On one occasion a particular runner returned to report to the commander. "Well, how does it look?" he was asked. The runner, an irrepressible optimist, replied enthusiastically, "We can attack in any direction, sir. We're surrounded!"

As comedienne Lily Tomlin quipped in her one-woman show, "No matter how cynical I get, I can't keep up."

We live in a time of issues explosions as we confront the crisis of the week screaming at us from our TV sets or print headlines or computer screens. There is too much to do, too much information to absorb, and too long a wait between action and result; the world seems terribly out of control. What results is a sense of rage, helplessness, or despair. The mind is numbed, the spirit sinks, and like Voltaire's Candide, we respond to a world of evil by cultivating our gardens.

To make matters worse, we hear a glowing paean of praise for the great economic recovery of the nineties, while over thirty million of our fellow citizens are trapped in poverty, one in four of them a child. We are seduced by the machinations of Wall Street and economic statistics that do as much to obfuscate reality as to clarify it. Homophobia, sexism, classism, racism, ableism, and ageism are stubbornly powerful forces in our midst. While the Third World is mired in debt and hunger, while the gap between rich and poor increases both within and between nations, while civil war rages in Europe, Africa, and Southeast Asia, and our cities decay, we are assured it is the best of all possible worlds and will only get better.

We live in a time when compassion is regarded as mere sentimentality, if not with contempt. The sense of community has been shattered, private utilitarianism has overwhelmed public spirit, and citizenship means lobbying for lower personal and corporate taxes, not striving for the common good. We are confronted with what Robert Bellah calls in *Habits of the Heart* "a cancerous individualism which infects citizens as it neglects the commonweal." Harvard's Robert D. Putnam has summarized his concern for declining social engagement and trust in his "bowling alone" thesis. He worries that with the passing from the scene of what he calls "the long civic generation," those born between 1910 and 1940, there has been a steady decline in social and political participation. While his thesis is hotly debated, I believe he is fundamentally correct. And if he is, then our concern for the generations born after 1940 must be great. The "I" of individualism has not matured into the "WE" of membership in a community. More anecdotal is the report of a speaker at a municipal service club who addressed the group under the ironic title "The Common Good: What's In It for Me?"

This fairly represents the tenor of the times, its zeitgeist. Meanwhile, increasing numbers of persons, Unitarian Universalists among them, try to live joyfully, seek significance, and create meaning in their lives as people heaven-bent for justice. They find it impossible to be totally happy sitting on an island of plenty in the midst of a rising sea of poverty.

Unitarian Universalists, I believe, share a religious conviction that history is a human project in which we are both the changers and the changed. Like the creative minority of which historian Arnold Toynbee wrote, we seek to transform the world and at the same time find ourselves transformed by it. We might liken ourselves and others like us to the biblical saving remnant, which sought to keep alive the flame of justice even in the face of massive injustice. I believe that our religious tradition provides us not only tools for theological and ethical analysis, not only a moral frame of reference, but also the resources to emerge from the slough of despond and do what Eric Lindeman calls the "humdrum work of democracy." Neither liberal religion nor democracy is a spectator sport. It will not be easy. Whether we understand God as precisely the source of unrest in the world, as one who sides with the poor, or whether our liberation theology is couched in terms of religious humanism, it is clear there are no cosmic lifeguards who will save us from ourselves.

The chapel of Staunton Harold in Leicestershire, England, was built in the seventeenth century, when civil war had ravaged the land and all hope everywhere was at its lowest ebb. On one of the walls of the chapel there is a tablet bearing this inscription: "In the year 1653, when all things were throughout the nation either demollisht or profaned, Sir Robert Shirley, Barronet, founded this church. Whose singular praise it is to have done the best things in the worst times and hoped them in the most calamitous."

In a sense, all of us are called to the work of justice. Who or What calls us we cannot be sure. Whether it be God, or History, or Humanity, we do not know for a certainty. We only know for sure that we are called, as was the prophet Isaiah in the temple. "Here I am, send me!"

CHAPTER TWO

Confessions of
a Militant Mystic

In the Roman Mass there is a frequent exchange between priest and people: One morning, according to the social action magazine *The Witness*, it went like this: "The Lord be with you," to which the congregation replied, "and with you also." And so it went until an ecclesiastical/technological gremlin did something to the pulpit microphone. Frustrated, the priest said, "There's something wrong with the mike," to which the well-trained congregation dutifully replied, "and with you also."

There is not only something wrong with him and but also with the world. Noting this, I have found deep meaning in the Hebrew phrase *Tikkun ha' olam*, repair of the world, for surely the world, wonderful as it is, is broken. In his essays, Emerson said there is "a crack in everything God has made." I submit that one of the central missions of the Unitarian Universalist movement is trying to fix these cracks, repairing the world and creating the Beloved Community of Love and Justice. The inner urge to work in the service of this vision I call the prophetic imperative, the sewing together of spirituality and social action as a seamless garment.

DEFINING THE TERMS

I use *confession* not as in the private act of admitting sin, "missing the mark" in Hebrew, but as a public confession of personal theology—articulating one's convictions, with no attempt to convert, but merely to inform.

Militant. I am not by nature pugnacious; I am a relatively gentle and mild-mannered soul. However, increasingly I experience an explosion of righteous indignation at injustice, an anger that I believe was in those biblical prophets who condemned injustice. In professing ethical monotheism, they believed God cared more about justice than ritual and whispered as much into their ears. Believing they were mouthpieces of God, their coda was "Thus saith the Lord." I share their anger at injustice, though not their acute sense of hearing.

By *mystic* I mean one sensitive to a reality greater than the self, but of which the self is an integral part. Believing that self is enmeshed in ultimate reality, the mystic celebrates that serendipitous union. It has similarly been suggested by Gerhard von Rad in the May 23, 1979, *Christian Century* that the prophet is "one who participates in the emotions of God," a seemingly presumptuous claim for a religious humanist like myself. However, making use of the image articulated by the late Angus H. MacLean in *The Wind in Both Ears,* I try imaginatively to take a "God's eye view of the world," seeking to distance myself, however slightly, from my human predicament, to identify with the highest cosmic good insofar as I can imagine that good. In this sense I am a mystic, with a prophetic twist.

Spirituality is a current buzz word in the culture—soul has gone mainstream—but it is reflective of dimensions of experience that transcend the utilitarian, recognizing that there is more to living than eye can see, hand can touch, ear can hear, nostrils can inhale, words can say. Spiritual has to do with soul, that which is irreducible in us, an understanding that we are both *homo faber,* the working animal, and *homo spiritus,* the religious creature. We are the ones about whom there is no bottom line. People are not cost-effective. We are both a deep well of faith and a teeming river of action that cannot be quantified.

Social action is a much-beleaguered term that simply means justice making, repairing a broken world. In Annie Dillard's fortuitous phrase in *Pilgrim at Tinker Creek,* we are admonished "to keep the world from falling apart." Social action comes from a spiritual recognition that we are as much members as individuals. We are citizens of a human community as well as centers of personal consciousness. Convictions have consequences.

Seamless garment is a term used in other contexts to suggest ethical consistency. For me, it is a realization that trying to separate the spiritual from the social is a meaningless, if not dangerous, enterprise. I challenge the seeming contradiction between prayer and politics, contemplation and action, being and doing. We should not talk about putting faith into action or religion into practice as if faith did not include action or religion, practice. Spiritual and social are in a dialogue so interwoven it is hard to distinguish the one from the other.

There is a biblical example of this unfortunate attempt. In the Gospel of Matthew's Sermon on the Mount, Jesus says "Blessed are the poor in spirit, for theirs is the kingdom of heaven." But in the Sermon on the Plain in Luke, the Social Gospel, Jesus says "Blessed are ye poor, for yours is the kingdom of God." Either Matthew has spiritualized the social gospel of Luke or Luke has socialized the spiritual gospel of Matthew. The social without the spiritual is rudderless; the spiritual without the social is vacuous. Matthew and Luke should have gotten together.

EVERYTHING BEGINS IN MYSTICISM AND ENDS IN POLITICS

In short, life is our only chance to both grow a soul and repair the world. We cannot really do one without the other. Ultimately, mystic and prophet should be one. Here I use militant as the adjective, mystic as the noun. Mystical sensibility prompts prophetic passion. They fuel one another, questioning and informing each other. As the French spiritual and political leader Charles Peguy wrote at the turn of the century, "Everything begins in mysticism and ends in politics."

Nor was Peguy alone in this thought. Paul Tillich in his *Theology of Culture* once said, "There is no vacuum in spiritual life, as there is no vacuum in nature. An ultimate concern must express itself socially." Karl Barth urged Christians to carry a Bible in one hand and a newspaper in the other. Dag Hammarskjold wrote in *Markings* that "The road to holiness necessarily passes through the world of action." And in *On Being Human Religiously,* James Luther Adams taught us that "The 'holy' thing in life is the participation in those processes that give body and form to universal justice." Our spiritual values must express themselves in the world of powers and principalities.

Poet Marge Piercy compared the pitcher crying out for water to a person crying out for work that is real. The urgency of the prophetic imperative under which I live is dictated by what happens to me in the holy quiet of this hour. This can create quite a problem. My life's task is trying to resolve the dilemma posed so exquisitely by essayist E. B. White, who arose in the morning "torn between the desire to improve the world and a desire to enjoy the world. This makes it hard to plan the day." Or, I would add, to plan a life. To savor the world or to serve it? I have concluded that to savor we *must* serve; in serving we *do* savor. In more traditional theological language, we are at the same time both vessels and instruments of God.

It has been said that mysticism begins in mist and ends in schism. There is a mistiness about mysticism that can be downright mushy, murky, muddy. Yet who among us can deny those all-too-infrequent experiences when, in poet Wallace Stevens's terms, we experience "times of inherent excellence"? In Tillich's word, we are "grasped" by something beyond ourselves.

A PERSONAL PERSPECTIVE

I was called to enter the ministry when I was a Boy Scout at the 1951 National Jamboree in the historic hills of Valley Forge, Pennsylvania. As an impressionable country lad of fourteen, with fifty thousand youth from around the world, I heard General Dwight D. Eisenhower and President Harry S. Truman on successive nights. Having been born a Universalist and brought up in a Universalist church school, I was well-prepared soil for what seed might drop. It was planted by a Methodist bishop from Indiana who one memorable Sunday morning issued a sermonic call to serve humanity.

Today, I would no doubt classify that sermon as sentimental, if not maudlin, but then and there I heard what I presumed to be the voice of God calling me to ministry. With some sadness I confess I have not heard that voice nearly so clearly since. However, it was of sufficient urgency at the time that it has directed the course of my life. It was a mystical call to action. "Here I am, send me."

Father Thomas Merton felt called to the monastery to escape the world and encounter God. Instead, he found himself, not farther from the world, but drawn ever closer to it. "There is always a temptation," he wrote, "to diddle around in the contemplative life, making itsy-bitsy statues." In his classic *Conjectures of a Guilty Bystander*, he describes a transformative experience that occurred one day on a city street:

> In Louisville, at the corner of Fourth and Walnut, in the center of the shopping district, I was suddenly overwhelmed with the realization that I loved all those people, that they were mine and I theirs, that we could not be alien to one another even though we were total strangers. It was like waking from a dream of separateness, of spurious self-isolation in a special world, the world of renunciation and supposed holiness. The whole illusion of a separate holy existence is a dream. . . . This sense of liberation from an illusory difference was such a relief and such a joy to me that I almost laughed out loud. . . . To think that such a commonplace realization should suddenly seem like news that one holds the winning ticket in a cosmic sweepstakes. . . . if only everybody could realize this! But it

cannot be explained. There is no way of telling people that they are all walking around shining like the sun.

There are experiences that come to me quite unbidden, when I am overwhelmed by just such a feeling—first what the late Joseph Campbell called in *The Power of Myth* "the rapture of being alive," and then a poignant sense of compassion for all people, especially those troubled in body or spirit, who live in oppression and poverty. And while I can make an intellectual case for spiritual and ethical concern for the other, it is these moments of identification with what is human and good that take me outside myself, and I join what Albert Schweitzer in his essay "Retrospect and Prospect" called "the fellowship of those who bear the mark of pain."

After all, is not one of the purposes of religion to overcome the excesses of ego? The mystic accomplishes this by union with the All; the activist by serving the Other. "To be is to be for others" said theologian Gene Reeves. I find a striking correspondence between the two paths to heightened spiritual experience.

Where Spiritual and Social Meet

We tend to think of the spiritual as private—that personal and untouchable zone of the soul whence comes our strength. Social responsibility, on the other hand, is public, what we do in the world. This is a necessary, but not sufficient, understanding. Some suggest the two are not only different, but opposite. My personal experience contradicts that unfortunate bifurcation. Spiritual implies power, and personal power needs to be expressed in a public way. Social action is not so much a product of my faith, but one of its dimensions, absolutely essential to my spiritual health. I could no more ignore justice-making and remain outside the public realm than I could absent myself from Sunday worship and retreat into myself. Promotion of justice, equity, and compassion in human relations is as vital as acceptance of one another and encouragement to spiritual growth in our congregations. Neglect of either is unthinkable—heretical. In the words of the old Russian proverb, "Pray to God, but row for the shore."

Spirituality is overcoming our narcissism, our preoccupation with a nonstop celebration of self. Self-interest has shaped our moral convictions almost exclusively. The consumer society is devoid of meaning; shopping has been called by Ernest Becker in *The Denial of Death* a form of mental illness. In a materialistic age, happiness recedes even as we prosper. The self-indulgent life has become a spiritual bore. The ideal union of the spiritual and the social is a mingling of the two in a stance that has been called that of the "militant mystic," to use Adam Curle's phrase.

I submit that public life is an arena of religious experience. If we deprive ourselves of it, we lose a great opportunity for spiritual growth. The word *public* is, after all, derived from the same word as puberty, both suggesting movement into adulthood. We might even view the social/ethical expression of the spiritual in terms of Erik Erikson's generative stage as articulated in *Childhood and Society*. "Generativity," he writes, "is primarily the interest in establishing and guiding the next generation. . . ." This is in contrast with self-regarding obsession with the private sphere of existence, which he calls stagnation. A purely private spirituality leads to a withering of the self, checking our pulses instead of our responsibilities. Preoccupation with the private is stultifying. The Greek word *idiot* means a private person, one who does not hold public office, hence an ignorant individual, since all intelligent citizens were expected to hold office at some point in their lives.

Social justice work is simply a natural spiritual evolution. Mystical and militant inclinations need one another. Social responsibility has too much centrifugal force; it needs to be balanced by the centripetal pull of inward spiritual experience to bring us back to the center from which the wholeness comes. To change the figure, the warp of the spiritual and the weft of the social form a vibrant pattern, a seamless garment of being and doing.

It was probably William James's classic *Varieties of Religious Experience* that has led us to believe that religious experience is confined to the mystical. I believe James did not pay enough attention to religious experience that has an ethical component.

I think of one of the transformative moments of my life, which combined the mystical and the ethical. The year was 1965, the height of the civil rights struggle. I was a graduate student in social ethics at the University of Chicago Divinity School. After three years in a suburban Cleveland church, I had made enough mistakes as an activist that I decided to go to school to learn how it ought to be done. I learned, almost too late, the truth of the Turkish proverb, "If you must speak the truth, have a fast horse and one foot in the stirrup of the saddle."

Martin Luther King, Jr., was conducting a voter rights campaign in Selma, Alabama. The Reverend James Reeb of All Souls Church (Unitarian) in Washington, D.C., was murdered on those hate-filled streets, and Unitarian Universalists were urged to gather for the memorial service at which Martin Luther King, Jr., was to speak. I dropped my studies briefly and flew to Atlanta from where, in the dark of night, we were led in a car caravan to Selma. After we arrived early the next day, we marched nervously through a cordon of Alabama troopers armed with long truncheons, which they pounded into their hands with intimidating force. Despite the fact that we were unarmed and at their physical mercy, I felt like a member of a liberating army as we approached the Brown's Chapel compound to be greeted by the cheers of the black residents and their supporters.

That afternoon I could not get into the sanctuary so great was the crush of bodies, and so I stood in an anteroom behind the pulpit, unable to see, but well able to hear. Then there was a stir behind me and Martin Luther King, Jr., brushed my arm on his way to the pulpit, our only meeting. His eloquent eulogy and the singing of "We Shall Overcome" with a cantorial descant of the Jewish prayer for the dead were simply overwhelming, and I was bathed in tears.

It was a mystical moment, calling to mind Theodore Parker's words that "the arc of the moral universe is long, but it bends toward justice." I felt myself a participant in the very making of history. I experienced a feeling of oneness with those worshippers of every race and religion—shirt-sleeve farmers with sweat on their faces, nuns in full habit, clergy in every imaginable liturgical garb. I knew then that my life would never be quite the same—and it wasn't.

When I returned to Chicago, I tried to resume work on an academic paper, "The Transformative Role of the Church in the Thought of H. Richard Niebuhr," a gripping title! But I found it hard to write. I wanted to speak. I wanted to be in a pulpit to share my experience! When my wife came home from work that evening, I said that I wanted to end my academic career; I wanted to go back into the parish ministry, where the action was. And so I did, never to regret it. Thus I date my birth as a militant mystic as March 15, 1965.

It may seem strange that a religious humanist uses God language, albeit poetically. Such a problem reminds me of the story of the priest and the peasant. The priest had come calling and admired the peasant's garden. "You and the Lord have done fine work here," said the good father. "Yes," replied the peasant. "You should have seen it when the Lord had it alone."

The Militant Mystic

Here is where mysticism enters the picture. With Unitarian Universalist theologian Henry Nelson Wieman, I think of the divine as the power of cosmic creativity. This creativity is manifest in nature as creative evolution; it is observed in history in those prophets of the human spirit who have tried to bend the arc of history toward justice against all odds; it is manifest here and now as we are co-creators of the Beloved Community. This work I know will not be completed in my lifetime, but I wish to work at repairing the world while I may. It is my mystic identification with this creative process that prompts me to continue.

There is a reality greater than ourselves, as James Luther Adams says in *On Being Human Religiously*, an "inescapable, commanding, reality that sustains and transforms all meaningful existence." While it transcends us ontologically, we are part and parcel of it, co-creators with it in a limited but vitally important way. This power speaks to me from people of prophetic fire, a creative minority who believe they can change the world; it speaks to me from the lives of ordinary men and women and children; and from the depths of my own heart when I pause long enough and thoughtfully enough to hear and heed.

The deeper that we delve into the innermost recesses of our souls, the more intensely we identify with other human beings. The further inward we explore, the more we see our common humanity. The more the unseen moves us, the more we understand the hidden bonds of community. And so the deeper we probe spiritually, the more we identify with others and cast our lot with them in battling all that keeps us from celebrating our mystic bonds. This is my passionate and enduring center.

The mystic oneness has been given eloquent and poetic articulation by the late David Rhys Williams in *We Speak of Life:*

> We are joined together by a mystic oneness whose source we may never know, but whose reality we can never doubt. . . . This mystic oneness . . . has been glimpsed by nearly all the great seers and leaders of humanity. We are our neighbor's keeper, because that neighbor is but our larger self. . . . Behold, thou shalt love thy neighbor as thyself, because thy neighbor is thyself.

I find that the term *Beloved Community* is a humanistically oriented substitute for *Kingdom of God*, deftly finessing issues of sexism, patriarchy, and theology and creating a poetic metaphor to describe, not theological salvation in the next world, but social salvation in this.

Salvation is a word to set Unitarian Universalist teeth on edge. Salvation by faith: Martin Luther held that faith is the quintessential religious gesture; we are saved by the gracious love of God acting through Jesus Christ. Salvation by works: others believed doing good is the *sine qua non* of religion; one could earn one's way into heaven. Unitarian Universalist salvation by character was this-worldly social salvation by people of integrity, a consonance of inner and outer person whose convictions are embodied in good works.

There is a story told by Joel Anderle in the December 15, 1993, issue of *Context* about Martin Luther that underscores my belief that ethics is near the heart of religious experience. "After living what he believed to be a grace-full, faith-filled life, a Lutheran dies and finds himself baffled by the heat and flames of the afterlife. He gasps to another Lutheran through clouds of sulfur, "It's not exactly the way we pictured Heaven would be, is it?"

"No," his acquaintance replies. "Let's go ask Brother Martin to explain this supposed 'Paradise.'"

They find the still portly Martin Luther, alone and sweating profusely, and ask him what went wrong. Luther pauses, sighs, and says with resignation, "It was works."

Yes, it is works, but also faith: it is mystical and it is prophetic. If the primordial religious gesture is dependence that fuels gratitude, then our modest attempt to repair the world comes because we have been filled to overflowing with life and find it cannot be contained within the skin of our bodies or the circumference of our souls. If religion begins in thanksgiving, it ends in service. The soul shrivels if it loses its connectedness with other souls, with humanity and history and with that great cosmic context in which we live and move and have our being for too few precious years.

In *Markings*, Dag Hammarskjold wrote that "Only what you have given is salvaged from the nothing which will someday have been your life."

I am admittedly a Puritan, one who is constantly worried that someone, somewhere, somehow is having a good time. There is a bit of justification by works in me. One of my recurrent dreams, archetypal I am sure, is facing a final exam, suddenly remembering that I forgot to study. This perennial panic can wake me from a deep and peaceful slumber. I am sure life has a final exam somewhere; I am not sure where or when or who administers it, or what the criteria are, or what the consequences of passing or failing might be. But I know there is one. Most likely I am the one who administers it.

I think back in our own history to the seventeenth-century Minor Church of Poland. To an impressive degree its adherents stressed church discipline, by which they meant the frequent reminding of individuals of their duty as faithful people in a religious community. Quarterly, a moral and spiritual examination was made of each member, followed by exhortation and correction from minister and laity alike. It was serious business, and each had to make an accounting of his or her stewardship. Such an interview was no doubt the precursor of our Ministerial Fellowship Committee! A Catholic historian later declared this religious faith was very influential in Polish history, and that one reason why its adherents did not become more numerous was that its moral and spiritual demands were too strict.

How Do Unitarian Universalists Measure Up?

How do we measure up as a movement of both mystics and prophets? For some time now I have had a lover's quarrel with our movement. When I was a graduate student at Colgate Rochester Divinity School, a fellow student, a Catholic Worker priest, knowing I was working on the prophetic imperative in Unitarian Universalism, asked me point-blank—"How can your denomination—middle class as it is—critique the system that has so favored it?" It was a disturbing question. I have been troubled by his implied accusation ever since.

There is a temptation among us to be complacent. This is our default mode, we who have been called the technicians and bureaucrats of the establishment. By and large we benefit from the status quo. "Come weal, come woe, my status is quo" is too often our mantra. How, then, can we exhibit the prophetic zeal to envision what might and ought to be, much less be in the vanguard of those who seek to bring that vision to reality? In biblical terms, Unitarian Universalists tend to be "terribly at ease in Zion." As Clarence Skinner once lamented, "A stuffed prophet sees no visions."

This relative complacency is as much a spiritual as a social problem. Who are we religiously, and what are the meanings that guide our lives? How does the quest for justice play out in our quest for meaning—the age-old religious enterprise? In short, what is our religious mission statement? My attempt to create one for myself goes as follows: "In the love of beauty and the spirit of truth, we unite for the celebration of life and the service of humanity." This is my faith as a militant mystic, a spiritual core coupled with an ethical imperative. By themselves, neither of these values can survive. They must stand together or the whole thing will fall apart.

The church, then, is a school of the spirit, helping us to probe the depths of worship and work. It is a locus, and perhaps the only locus, where we can ask the basic questions of the meaning of our brief guest appearance on this earthly stage.

Living in the New Millennium under the Prophetic Imperative

In this new millennium we will need to do some serious soul-searching and world repairing—the two go hand in hand. We of the liberal religious faith are slowly, but steadily, being marginalized, overwhelmed by a confident fundamentalist political theology that threatens to engulf us utterly. However disparagingly we may speak of the Religious Right, it has tapped into something very deep; it has given its followers a spiritual rootedness in a dogmatic faith and a sense of purpose grounded in an absolutist politics.

We who eschew dogma and reject absolutism will need to work harder than the denizens of the Right, for our faith demands more of us. We need the power of conviction even in the face of our ultimate uncertainty about the nature of reality and right and wrong. While it is perhaps better to be vaguely right than absolutely wrong, the very nature of our faith requires of us deeper convictions.

The times are dire, but then people who live under the prophetic imperative are always worried. I am hopeful, though not optimistic, about our capacity to repair the world in the face of the many unjust assaults upon it. In such a situation I am encouraged by the Hebrew prophet Jeremiah who, even as he warned of imminent doom and approaching foreign invasion, bought a piece of land as a sign and symbol of hope. So must we all.

Theologian Leonard Sweet recounts a story about the German poet Heinrich Heine, who stood with a friend before the cathedral of Amiens in France.

"Tell me, Heinrich," said his friend, "why can't people build piles like this any more?"

Replied Heine, "My dear friend, in those days people had convictions. We moderns have opinions. And it takes more than opinions to build a Gothic cathedral."

And it takes more than opinions to build the Beloved Community of Love and Justice. It will take a cadre of militant mystics whose gratitude for living is so pervasive that it overflows into the social life. Spirituality and social action are a seamless garment—a coat of many colors.

CHAPTER THREE

Meriting the
Wind We Inherit

Tradition has it that, while revolution was raging in St. Petersburg in 1917, a convocation of the Russian Orthodox Church was in session a few blocks away engaged in bitter debate over what color vestments their priests should wear. Any religious movement that succumbs to trivialization, that ignores the times in which it lives, is sure to be damned by history, and deservedly so. The Unitarian Universalist movement is not immune to such temptations.

Do we merit the wind we inherit? In the play by Jerome Lawrence and Robert E. Lee, *Inherit the Wind,* the Scopes monkey trial is dramatized. The protagonist for the biblical version of creationism and development, Brady (William Jennings Bryant in the trial), invokes a verse from Proverbs: "He who troubles his household will inherit the wind." Troublemakers tend to get their historical just deserts. Liberal religion has been troubling the household of faith for over four centuries. It is time to learn what it is that we have inherited and what we might do to merit it. Have we been socially responsible?

William Ellery Channing set down the first principle of Unitarian Universalist social responsibility, religion as a social principle, in an 1820 sermon at the Federal Street Church.

> Religion, we are told, is a private, personal thing, a concern between the individual and God. His neighbor or the community must not meddle with it. . . . I would maintain that religion is eminently a social principle, entering into social life, as having most important bearings on the public weal. . . . The social character of religion is not sufficiently regarded.

I contend that (1) Unitarian Universalism as a movement has continually resisted the religion of purely personal piety, insisting that religion is a social principle as well; (2) there has been a steady transition from a service-oriented, primarily charitable emphasis toward a focus on systemic change; and (3) the institutional church as a voluntary association has taken and ought to take an increasing role in the quest for social justice.

THE EIGHTEENTH CENTURY

In the eighteenth century there were intimations that religious liberals were concerned as much with the public as the private weal. The Reverend Charles Chauncey (1705–1787) was minister of Boston's First Church for sixty years, during which time he was a powerful advocate of liberty for the Colonies. The Reverend Jonathan Mayhew (1720–1766), minister of West Church in Boston, has been called the father of civil and religious liberty in Massachusetts and America, preaching civil disobedience toward King George during the Revolutionary period.

In the Universalist tradition, too, there were those who intermingled their religion and their politics. Elhanan Winchester (1751–1797) believed universal salvation mandated that he baptize blacks. One of his followers, Dr. Benjamin Rush (1745–1813), was a signer of the Declaration of Independence, founder of the first hospital for the mentally ill, organizer of the first antislavery society in America, promoter of the public school, and the father of American psychiatry. John Murray (1741–1815) founded the Gloucester Universalist Church with Gloster Dalton, an African slave, as a charter member. He also successfully resisted the taxing power of the state for the support of religion and led the congregation in withholding taxes from the established church so that they might contribute voluntarily to the Universalist Church. Dr. George de Benneville (1703–1793) was a medical missionary among Native Americans.

The intimate relationship of politics and religion in the new nation is illustrated in the tradition of the Election Sermon, in which Unitarians and Universalists figured heavily. It was a tradition inaugurated by the Reverend John Cotton in 1634, at which time he urged Governor Winthrop's reelection. The tradition continued almost unbroken, usually at the opening session of the Massachusetts General Court when the Governor's Council was chosen. This event, held in May, became the occasion for annual meetings of many voluntary associations, including the May Meetings of the American Unitarian Association. Channing's sermon "Spiritual Freedom" was the election sermon in 1830. The Universalist president of Tufts College, Dr. A. A.

Miner, delivered the last Election Sermon in 1884. While these sermons were not openly partisan, they were not full of innocuous generalizations. They made pointed suggestions about how government should comport itself. Prior to the American Revolution, they discussed the political theory of John Locke and thus laid the groundwork for revolt.

John Adams (1735–1826), one of the two Founding Fathers who was avowedly a Unitarian (Jefferson was the other), wrote these words about politics and religion in his book *In God We Trust: The Beliefs of the Founding Fathers:*

> Massachusetts is then seized with a violent fit of anger at the clergy. It is curious to observe the conduct of the Tories towards this sacred body. If a clergyman, of whatever character, preaches against the principles of the revolution . . . the Tories cry him up as an excellent man and a wonderful preacher. But if a clergyman preaches Christianity and tells the magistrates that they were not distinguished from their brethren for their private good but for the good of the people, that the people are bound in conscience to obey a good government, but are not bound to submit to one that aims at destroying all the ends of government—ho, sedition, treason! When the clergy engage in a political warfare, religion becomes a most powerful engine, either to support or overthrow the state.

These eighteenth-century figures and themes exemplify social service (De Benneville), social education (The Election Sermon), social witness (Chauncey) and social action (the antislavery society). There was a dawning consciousness of the need to organize for social action; yet, by and large, the organized church was not significantly engaged.

PRAGMATISM AND ACTIVISM

The late President John F. Kennedy, addressing a gathering of noted Americans at a White House Dinner, said: "No greater gathering of intelligence, talent, and skill has been assembled here since President Jefferson dined alone."

Thomas Jefferson (1743–1826) was a singular figure in American history. The tendency to express basic religious convictions in political action came to a culmination in him. He was an Anglican vestryman (though not long active) who once said, "I am content to be a Unitarian by myself." Although there were virtually no organized Unitarian churches in his day, Jefferson and John Adams often listened to the

Unitarian preacher, scientist, and activist Joseph Priestley (1733–1804) while they were in Philadelphia. Jefferson's personal religion could be called deistic and was viewed by many as heretical. But it is his social philosophy that is of prime interest here. Jefferson was a materialist; facts were of central importance. From the superb order of creation that God had made, people were to learn how to conquer the wilderness and order a new government. Human institutions must reflect nature; human beings were the architects of the new nation. Their God-given power to cope with nature was central; government should release, not restrict, that power. There was no place for creed or dogma in his faith, no role for metaphysics. He detested Plato, whom he called the "patron saint of abstraction."

Jefferson's philosophy of government was essentially framed by the physical realities of America. In a nation perched on the edge of a promising wilderness, there was not time for extended reflection or meditation. The American landscape uttered a simple call for action, and so the keynote of Jeffersonian thought simply became the American task: to explore the wilderness and create a new nation where people could flourish in freedom.

The same pragmatic strain that informed Jefferson's political philosophy informed his religion. This pragmatism has dominated American philosophy, and to a considerable extent American religion, ever since. While his theological deism captured only a few nineteenth-century Unitarians, his pragmatic philosophy was decisive in the emerging age of reform. Unitarians have long stressed salvation by character, and Jefferson's pragmatism must be seen as a powerful influence on the nation in general and religious liberals in particular.

Jefferson, then, sets the tone for Unitarian Universalist social responsibility, eschewing excessive introspection as a depletion of energy and concentrating on social action. He was of the aristocracy, yet his political philosophy championed the cause of the masses of people. This philosophy set the stage for the great reforms of the nineteenth century.

THE NINETEENTH-CENTURY AGE OF REFORM

The "colossus of American Unitarianism" was William Ellery Channing (1780–1842), for forty years minister of the Federal Street Society (later the Arlington Street Church) in Boston. He was both the theological leader of Unitarian Christianity and a pivotal figure in the rapidly emerging age of reform. By upbringing and marriage he was distinctly upper middle class. Yet experiences in his development were to prompt him to attack the very establishment that both spawned and supported him. Critical among these was a year and a half spent in Richmond, Virginia, where he came into contact with slavery side by side with patrician wealth.

As a reformer he was continually torn by his drive for reconciliation instead of conflict; his was an ivory tower temperament, driven by the reformer's force of will. He believed in personal moral regeneration, yet he found himself drawn into structural reform; he was a patrician who was drawn to associate with commoners. He was, as Jack Mendelsohn points out in his book of the same title, a "reluctant radical."

Channing illustrates several dimensions of the prophetic imperative. He was a prophet in his own time, dropping the plumbline of his nineteenth-century Christian liberalism over the young nation. Although not a pacifist, he was opposed to U.S. entry into the War of 1812. In the aftermath of that war he worked with fellow Unitarian Noah Worcester (1758–1837) to form the Massachusetts Peace Society in 1815. It was open to pacifists and nonpacifists alike. In opposition to the Mexican War, he wrote an impassioned essay in 1841, just a year before his death, inquiring, "Has the duty of obeying government no bounds?"

For him, it had—the bounds of conscience. Channing was also a staunch defender of freedom of the press. He successfully fought for the right to use Faneuil Hall in Boston for a protest rally on behalf of the martyred publisher Elijah Lovejoy in 1837. He was a member of the Boston School Board and was active in numerous other groups and causes. Perhaps Channing's greatest significance, however, can be found in the impact he had on other reformers. Historian Edith Abbott, in an unpublished and thus oft-neglected essay, writes, "Channing's place in the social reform movement of his day can perhaps best be described by saying that he was a leader of great leaders."

Channing inspired Horace Mann, a congregant, in his efforts to found a public school system in Massachusetts and Antioch College in Ohio. He encouraged Dorothea Dix in her work with the imprisoned and the insane. Dr. Samuel Gridley Howe, developer of methods for teaching the blind, deaf, and mentally retarded, was a follower of Channing. Julia Ward Howe, feminist and author of the "Battle Hymn of the Republic," was also inspired by his ministry. Channing suggested Joseph Tuckerman, "Dr. Channing's field marshall in action," for appointment as "Boston's minister to the poor," which became the Benevolent Fraternity of Unitarian Churches, now the Boston Urban Ministry. Channing prodded abolitionist Senator Charles Sumner, a fellow Unitarian, in his efforts. His parishioner Elizabeth Peabody brought the kindergarten to this country. In all this, however, he did make enemies: the conservative Daniel Webster of his own congregation, Henry Clay, and John C. Calhoun, another Unitarian of conservative bent.

Channing operated from a sense of a religious imperative to ameliorate the injustice of society. It may be said that this imperative was nothing but a sense of duty, of *noblesse oblige,* of one well born are great things expected. "Every man whom God has prospered is bound to contribute to this work," Channing said at a meeting of the Benevolent Fraternity. In a lecture on Joseph Tuckerman, he uttered this challenge: "God has prospered us, in our business; let us show our gratitude by inquiring for what end prosperity is given, and how it may best accomplish the end of the Giver. Let us give a high character to our city."

There was also a dawning understanding of the Beloved Community, an interdependent society in which social responsibility was a key ingredient. Religion could never remain mere piety. In response to the objection that our sole duty is to care for ourselves and family, that we do not have time to care for others, he wrote of the great waste of time in trivial pursuits, the energy squandered in minutia that could be better spent in redeeming society from evil. Such a commitment would not compromise our domestic duties.

Although Channing stands tall as an individual reformer, it is unquestionably true that he believed in an institutional response to social problems. Channing, according to James Luther Adams, wrote the first systematic essay on the nature and role of voluntary associations, citizen groups organized to create social change. In this essay, a report to the American Unitarian Association, he wrote of the disposition,

> to form associations to accomplish all objects by organized masses. . . . You can scarcely name an object for which some institution has not been formed. Would men spread one set of opinions or crush another? Then make a society. Would they improve the penal code, or relieve poor debtors? They make societies. Would they encourage agriculture, or manufactures or science? They make societies. Would one class encourage horse racing, and another discourage traveling on Sunday? . . . Men can do jointly what they cannot do singly. . . . In truth the great object of all benevolence is to give power, activity and freedom to others.

This approach he believed served both social and personal values. It accumulated power by union, and it enabled sincere persons to gain warmth and earnestness by association with other committed souls. The church was one among these voluntary associations that could empower others. He even attempted to persuade his church to create and fund a social action committee that would serve the poor, improve education, investigate prison conditions, and seek to find ways to prevent poverty.

To this end, an Association of the Members of the Federal Street Society for Benevolent Purposes was formed, with modest results. Although perhaps bordering on simple evangelism, Channing's work in the creation of the Benevolent Fraternity does illustrate the importance of institutional church response to need. Joseph Tuckerman ushered in a direct ministry to the poor which we might today call a street ministry or simple philanthropy. Tuckerman, however, was in many ways a conservative; he opposed the unionization of labor and all governmental activities on behalf of the poor, feeling private charity was equal to the task. While Tuckerman is thought to be a precursor of the Social Gospel movement, his style was typical of the period, a ministry to persons, not structures; social service, not social action. Channing, while stressing this ministry to individuals, was beginning to question the very structures of the society itself, although he did not fully grasp the nature of systemic change. Economist John E. MacNab, discussing the relationship between Unitarianism and socialism in this period, wrote in the 1953 *Proceedings* of the Unitarian Historical Society:

> The Unitarian, however, applying his rational approach to the problem becomes aware that society is no longer a simple entity, but an ever increasing complexity. Regardless of how well-intentioned and how wise men may be, they are prevented by the very grossness of mankind's relations from living peacefully and securely and justly. And, seeking to implement his belief in the brotherhood of man and a social gospel, he finds that there must be in both the political and economic fields an organized cooperative effort if injustice, insecurity and war are to be avoided.

And so Channing can be seen as one struggling through to that realization. His views on economic questions, for example, reveal both naiveté and insight, caution and courage. Channing held views of a communistic society and was opposed to private property; inveighed against those "maddened with wealth" who did not discharge their responsibility to the poor; worked with Boston's poor even while serving a prosperous church; raised large sums of money for charity, although he began to wonder why this society seemed to spawn so many charitable needs. He was torn between ministering to individual poor people and reforming the social conditions and institutions that kept them poor.

His basic ambivalence toward the poor and his patrician background are revealed in his sermon "Ministry for the Poor," given in 1835: "That some of the indigent among us die of scanty food is undoubtedly true; but vastly more in this community die from eating too much, than from eating too little; vastly more from excess, than starvation."

Yet he could also sound a great prophetic voice in opposition to the injustice of poverty. While his friend Joseph Tuckerman wanted to relieve the sufferings of pauperism, Channing wanted to abolish it. In his sermon on poverty he said, "Study this great social evil, its causes, its prevention, its cure, with full confidence that in society there is healing power, and that no evil is desperate except despair." Again, Channing can be seen as a reluctant radical.

The slavery issue, however, brought him excruciating inner turmoil. He had condemned slavery after his return from the West Indies in 1830. He was then accosted on the right by the solid merchants of his congregation whose textile businesses depended on slave labor. James T. Austin accused him of inciting a race war. Another merchant said he ought to stick to the gospel. On the left he was confronted by men like William Lloyd Garrison, who thought he was, as we would say, "pussyfooting through a revolution" with pious rhetoric and his consistent refusal to become a militant abolitionist. At last, under relentless pressure from people like Garrison, John Q. Adams, and Samuel J. May, he agreed he had been silent too long and joined the Abolitionist cause with a fury.

The conversation between Samuel J. May, minister of the Unitarian Church in Syracuse, New York, and Channing at the latter's house is indicative of his ambivalence and yet, at the same time, of his openness. May had been listening all evening to Channing's complaint that the abolitionists were too precipitate, that they lacked tact, that they were, in short, too violent. As described by Jack Mendelsohn in *Channing: The Reluctant Radical*, May, unable to control his impatience any longer, broke out:

> Dr. Channing, I am tired of these complaints. . . . It is not our fault that those who might have conducted this great reform

more prudently have left us to manage as we may. It is not our fault that those who might have pleaded for the enslaved so much more wisely and eloquently, both with pen and with the living voice, than we can have been silent. We are not to blame, sir, that you have not spoken. And now that inferior men have begun to speak and act against what you acknowledge to be an awful system in iniquity, it is not becoming in you to complain of us because we do it in an inferior style. Why, sir, have you not taken this matter in hand yourself?

Channing, unable to answer the rebuke, accepted the challenge, saying, "Brother May, I have been silent too long." He was later to say of the abolitionists, "The great interests of humanity do not lose their claims on us because sometimes injudiciously maintained."

By 1840, Channing became committed enough to lend the enormous prestige of his presence to the Convention of Friends of Universal Reform, a gathering that gave his fellow patricians apoplectic fits. Ralph Waldo Emerson said of it, "It was composed of madmen, madwomen, men with beards, Dunkers, Muggletonians, come-outers, Groaners, Agrarians, Seventh-Day Adventists, Quakers, Abolitionists, Calvinists, Unitarians and Philosophers."

Channing gradually came to see that moral passion directed toward individual change was not enough, and he advocated public action by voluntary groups. As he grew older he grew more radical, drawing away from his congregation and closer to the poor, the black, the working men, and the radicals. Symptomatic of this was his attempt to hold a memorial service for the abolitionist Charles Follen. Overruled by his governing board, he began to wonder about his usefulness to his church of forty years. He was never really dismissed, but he preached less and less often, and his long ministry simply petered out.

Channing stood out, with a handful in his day, against the essentially conservative bent of Unitarianism in the mid-nineteenth century. In *A History of Unitarianism in Transylvania, England, and America,* Earl Morse Wilbur characterized the majority as follows:

Belonging generally to the conservative class, socially and politically they were disposed to be complacent and self-confident, and they felt moved by no eager desire to make converts to their religion or to urge it upon others; but their main emphasis was upon uprightness of moral character; while they were given to philanthropic causes and the general welfare, were devoted to general interests, faithful to civic duties, and generous to cases of private need.

Channing, then, was of prophetic mold in declaring the imperative of religious social action. Characteristic of his class and day, he saw social problems in individual terms, although he began to have insights into the structural causes that rendered people poor and help-less. He utilized the vehicle of the church to send his parishioners into the community to live out religion as a social principle.

THEODORE PARKER: YANKEE CRUSADER

There were other reformers of Unitarian Universalist persuasion in the first half of the nineteenth century. Hosea Ballou (1771–1852) provided a theological articulation of universal salvation. The universal Father-hood of God was translated into an ethical principle, the universal Brotherhood of Man. Thomas Starr King (1824–1864), a militant aboli-tionist, raised vast sums of money for the National Sanitary Commis-sion during the Civil War and is credited with saving California for the Union. Abner Kneeland (1774–1844) was a Universalist minister known for having been convicted for blasphemy, but also for his founding of the cooperative community in Salubria, Iowa. Adin Ballou (1803–1890), another Universalist minister, was a devout pacifist and founder of the Hopedale Community. He influenced Tolstoy, who in turn influenced Mohandas Gandhi and Martin Luther King, Jr.

In the Unitarian tradition we might cite Henry David Thoreau (1817–1862) for his radical critique of society. However, this was done from without, not within, the church; it was social witness, not social action. Ralph Waldo Emerson (1803–1882) resigned his Unitarian pas-torate, saying that he was born with a seeing eye, not a helping hand. Later, in his American Scholar address, he said, "Action is with the scholar subordinate." Although he subsequently wrote and spoke in opposition to slavery, he maintained the view that to redeem society we must first redeem the individual. As Oliver Wendell Holmes once remarked, "It would have taken a long time to get rid of slavery if some of Emerson's teachings . . . had been accepted as the true gospel of liberty."

If Channing was a reluctant radical, Emerson a skeptic toward reform, and Thoreau a somewhat nonpolitical individualist, Theodore Parker (1810–1860) was none of these. A graduate of Harvard Divinity School, he accepted his first pastorate in West Roxbury, a congregation of common people. There he was both preacher and farmer, for the parish was small and the pay poor. His radical preaching, however, prompted a group of Boston gentlemen to resolve that "Theodore Parker should be heard in Boston," and he was. There was in Parker a mandate for Unitarians to engage themselves in their society.

In his "Sermon on Merchants" he urged his auditors to "Give the world more than you take." His extended letter to his congregation on his experiences as a minister contained this sentence: "The natural function of a great man is to help the little ones." "Christianity . . . makes a man's greatness consist in the amount of service he renders to the world," he observed in "Thoughts on Labor." Parker forcefully applied this imperative to himself as minister: "if the minister is to promote religion, he is to meddle with the state's business, the perishing classes, literature, science, morals, manners, everything that affects the welfare of mankind."

In the same work he compared the prophetic role of the minister with the priestly function, declaring that belief is inadequate and the most worthwhile worship is in a "sacrament of works." In his last letter to his congregation, printed in *Theodore Parker's Experience as a Minister,* Parker summarized his view of the prophetic ministry:

> So I have not only preached on the private virtues, which are and ought to be the most constant theme of all pulpits, but likewise on the public virtues that are also indispensable to the general welfare. . . . I have preached many political sermons. . . . No doubt I have often wounded the feelings of many of you. Pardon me, my friends. If I live long I doubt not that I shall do so again and again. You never made me your minister to flatter, or merely to please, but to instruct and serve.

The friends whom he may have wounded were members of the 28th Congregational Society, the Boston church he served from the time he left West Roxbury until illness forced his retirement. It was not merely the function of the minister to be prophetic; it was also the function of the whole church community. Feeling the church of his day was too often the caboose on the train of progress, Parker nonetheless determined to stay with it, albeit as a noisy gadfly. The churches of Boston were targets for his voice and pen. He accused them of being "as commercial as the shops," too often in the control of the "conservative element . . . which resists the further application of Christianity to public affairs" and dominated by merchants who were "backward in all reforms, excepting such as their own interest demands." He evidently thought the clergy were beholden to the merchants: "As a general rule, the clergy are on the side of power. . . . The clergy also are unconsciously bought up, their speech paid for, or their silence." He accused these clergy of "sitting drowsy in their Church of Commerce."

In the face of pressing social issues, "Is the church to say nothing, do nothing?" Parker asked as he called for the "church militant." If there are public sins, the church must give the alarm. It should be a "society for the promotion of good works." The church does this in two ways: first by addressing its own members and then the larger society. He went on to suggest a church organization that would address social injustice, a forerunner of social action committees.

> What if every Sunday afternoon the most pious and manly of our number, who saw fit, resolved themselves into a committee of the whole for practical religion, and held not a formal meeting, but one more free, sometimes for the purpose of devotion, the practical work of making ourselves better Christians, nearer to one another, and sometimes that we might find the means to help such as needed help, the poor, the ignorant, the intemperate, and the wicked.

Although he had hoped to pursue his scholarly endeavors while in Boston, the demands of his congregation and the problems of the age drove Parker from his study. As he flung himself passionately into the reforms of his day, his study at Exeter Place became a center for reformers. He became a conscience to his generation, the "best hated man in America," as he put it.

He discovered, however, that he could not simply attack one social evil at a time, for they were all of a piece. Sin was not so much an individual matter as the result of a society that victimized its people. As he reflected on his ministry, he came to see the inadequacy of charity and the need for justice.

> Yet it seemed to me the money given by public and private charity—two fountains that never fail in Puritanical Boston— was more than sufficient to relieve it all, and gradually remove the deep-seated and unseen cause which, in the hurry of business and of money, is not attended to. There is a hole in the dim-lit public bridge, where many fall through and perish. Our mercy pulls a few out of the water; it does not stop the hole, nor light the bridge, nor warn men of the peril! We need

the great Charity that palliates effects of wrong, and the greater Justice which removes the Cause.

His sophistication about the structural nature of society is revealed in a brief but seminal discussion of power, which James Luther Adams believes is the first systematic treatment of that subject by an American minister. Parker listed four major power configurations: commercial or trading power, political power, ecclesiastical power, and literary power (the colleges and the press). These were the forces that controlled society and with which any reformer must come to terms. In words more prophetic than he knew, he believed that commercial power dominated political power. "It can manufacture governors, senators, judges, to suit its purposes, as easily as it can make cotton cloth. . . . Your Congress is its mirror." He concluded simply, "Money is power."

Parker's analysis of poverty clearly indicates his growing realization of the need, not for charity, but for systemic change. In his "Sermon on Poverty," he discussed the causes of poverty: (1) the natural or organic cause emerging from geography, for example, or from want of power or body or mind of the people; (2) political suppression, which serves to concentrate wealth in the hands of the few; (3) social causes such as discrimination based on race. He recognized the poverty cycle. "The old poverty is parent of new poverty," he observed while criticizing the feeble efforts directed against poverty: "Poverty will not be removed till the causes thereof are removed. . . . we need both palliative charity and remedial justice." Parker went on to suggest specific remedies, such as tenements for the poor at low rent, which the churches should provide if the capitalists did not; enabling the poor to purchase food at low prices; and finding and creating jobs for them. He concluded, "The indiscriminate charity, which it is difficult to withhold from a needy and importunate beggar, does more harm than good."

Parker was something of a political leader as well. He was an unofficial advisor to the Free Soil and Republican parties. With a young Illinois lawyer named William Herndon, he kept a faithful correspondence on political questions. Once Parker sent Herndon two sermons on democracy, which contained these words: "The government of all, by all, and for all is a Democracy." Herndon liked Parker's preaching and passed these sermons along to his senior law partner, Abraham Lincoln, who underscored that particular passage.

It was on the question of slavery, however, that Parker's voice was most vehemently raised. He found he could not move the South; their economic interests and social habits made them invulnerable to a Yankee preacher. He then assailed New England, especially Daniel

Webster, who insisted that the purpose of government was to protect private property. "Southern slavery," Parker wrote, "is an institution which is in earnest. Northern freedom is an institution which is not in earnest." He formed a Vigilante Committee to help runaway slaves, many of whom he harbored in his home, keeping a loaded pistol on his desk to defend them. The passage of the Fugitive Slave Act in 1850 challenged Parker as both man and moralist. He reasoned that if truth came directly from God, if human concepts of truth were finite, then there must be a higher law for men to follow than the sometimes wicked laws of men. He determined to follow that higher law, disobey the act, and counsel others to do the same.

In so doing he incurred the wrath of many. During a religious revival at Park Street Church in Boston on March 6, 1858, the following prayer was uttered against Parker: "Lord, we know that we cannot argue him down, and the more we say against him, the more will people flock after him, and the more will they love and revere him. O Lord, O Lord, what shall be done for Boston if thou dost not take this and some other matters in hand."

Theodore Parker, then, exemplified the mandate for religious social action in a frenetic life of reform, which finally took its toll. He died in 1860 at the age of fifty. Parker used his church as a platform for his activism, taking many of his people with him into the community. He perceived the nature of power in the young nation and realized that economic interests were very much in the driver's seat. Parker well understood that "even small revolutions are not mixed with rosewater." He stands as the Unitarian Universalist prototype of a prophetic minister in a prophetic church.

Susan B. Anthony and the Spirit of Reform

Abigail Adams promised husband John on the eve of the American Revolution, "If particular care and attention is not paid to the Ladies, we are determined to foment a Rebellion." Women were prominent in Unitarian Universalist social reform movements from the beginning. Cynthia Grant Tucker documents the largely unknown story of spiritual nurture and social reform of women ministers in her *Prophetic Sisterhood: Liberal Women Ministers of the Frontier, 1880–1930*. In addition to supporting the reforms of the day, their very presence in the pulpit prompted a little girl in the Unity Church of Sioux Falls, South Dakota to cry out in a whisper heard by all, "Look, mama! There's a *man* up there in our pulpit." Another woman, not a minister, who carried out reforms was Charlotte Perkins Gilman (1860–1935), a utopian thinker and writer on economic justice, labor, and women's movements and an early and staunch advocate of the "child-garden" or day nursery to enable mothers to pursue careers. Probably even less well known is Frances Ellen Watkins Harper (1825–1911), a black woman and abolitionist. Serving as the superintendent of the colored branch of the Women's Christian Temperance Union (WCTU) and a vigorous opponent of WCTU's racism, she agonized over whether to support the Fifteenth Amendment enabling black men to vote, but not women of any race, or a women's suffrage amendment. In so doing she opposed the strategy of Elizabeth Cady Stanton and Susan B. Anthony, who zeroed in on women's suffrage, feeling that black suffrage would come later. It is to Susan B. Anthony (1820–1906) that we turn to discuss a systemic revolution in human rights.

In Mount Hope Cemetery in Rochester, New York stands the Anthony family monument with its four bold words carved in stone, "Liberty, Equality, Humanity, Justice," an apt summary of her religious convictions. Raised an orthodox Quaker, she joined the First Unitarian Church of Rochester on January 1, 1893. Finding the local meeting not in sympathy with the antislavery movement, the Anthony family and a number of other Quakers came to identify with the Unitarian Church. While Susan was teaching in Canajoharie, New York, to help support her family, her parents and sister Mary attended the first women's rights convention in Seneca Falls, New York, in 1848 (adjourned to the Rochester Unitarian Church) and signed its Declaration of Women's Rights. The convention had been called because women were excluded from antislavery deliberations.

Anthony worked with Frederick Douglass and the Underground Railroad. One diary entry indicates that she integrated her justice work into the details of daily existence: "Quilted all day, but sewing seems no longer my calling. . . . Fitted out a slave for Canada with help of Harriet Tubman." She became restive with what she called "the white orthodox male Saints," later a foil for her political consciousness. As a Daughter of Temperance, she spoke at a Sons of Temperance meeting although it was against the rules. When reprimanded, she stormed outside, followed by several women, her first spontaneous protest action. She formed the Woman's State Temperance Society and called a convention. She gravitated into women's suffrage because she felt that there would be no progress on the temperance front until women had the right to vote.

Her theology was clearly a pragmatic one. "I am tired of theory. I want to hear how we must act to have a happier and more glorious world." For example, in her famous interview with Nelly Bly she was asked, "Do you pray?" to which she answered, "I pray every single second of my life; not on my knees, but with my work. My prayer is to lift women to equality with men. Work and worship are one with me. I cannot imagine a God of the universe made happy by my getting down on my knees and calling him great."

Once, while speaking at a Universalist church convention, after her usual plea for woman's suffrage, she noted that there were no other women speakers on the platform: "I resent this from the bottom of my heart, and I demand of you to practice what you preach— Universalism." She was equally frank with her own Unitarian minister, William Channing Gannett. As former Rochester City historian Blake McKelvey noted, "She attended Dr. Gannett's sermons fairly regularly at this time, but her good friend never knew when a portion of his remarks would prompt enthusiastic praise or condemnation for some slight to women's rights."

Temperance work was the accepted public outlet for women's moral concerns, but it emphasized individual change without touching larger social issues. Anthony came to admire William Lloyd Garrison and Elizabeth Cady Stanton, five years her senior, whose concerns moved through the privatistic moral sphere to public morality. Stanton had helped pen the Declaration of Sentiments at the Seneca Falls Convention. Stanton, the intellectual of the women's rights movement, offered a new view of nineteenth-century woman.

Susan B. Anthony was not a mystic, but a pragmatist. Her personal theological convictions were important to the extent that they informed action on behalf of human liberation. For example, she defended the agnostic and rabble-rousing William Lloyd Garrison as the most Christ-like man she had ever known. After defeat in a women's suffrage vote in Colorado, she wrote somewhat bitterly of the reasons, many anchored in a biblical and sexist view of women: "There are, as you know, a few religious bigots left in the world who really believe that somehow or other if women are allowed to vote, Saint Paul would feel badly about it."

Her religious faith is best discovered through her deep sense of ethical responsibility. With the Universalist Clara Barton she formed the second Red Cross chapter in the nation, at Rochester in 1881. She was a pacifist, although torn by the Civil War until she uneasily justified it as a war for liberation. She practiced civil disobedience, urging defiance of the Fugitive Slave Act. Her bold act of voting in the presidential election of 1872 and her subsequent trial in Canandaigua must go down as one of the most dramatic cases of civil disobedience in American history.

Anthony opposed capital punishment, organizing rallies on behalf of the known, like John Brown, and the unknown, often at risk of life and limb. As a social radical writing and organizing on behalf of organized labor, especially for women, she was a friend of socialist Eugene Debs and a militant critic of the abuses of *laissez-faire* capitalism. She created women's groups and challenged men's control of the women's movement. Anthony began organizing women workers in 1868, linking the labor movement with women, an act which even Karl Marx noted.

Susan B. Anthony got into further trouble by harboring the abused wife of Senator Phelps from Massachusetts. "Trust me that as I ignore all law to help the slave, so will I ignore it all to protect the enslaved woman." It was during the 1850s that her thinking moved from private to political morality. Her organizing strategy was to choose a concrete issue, analyze the problem, formulate a specific demand, and then urge women to take practical, confrontational, and effective action based on the analysis. Biographer Kathleen Berry quotes her, in *Susan B. Anthony: A Biography of a Singular Feminist*, as warning,

> Cautious, careful people, always casting about to preserve their reputation and social standing, never can bring about a reform. Those who are really in earnest must be willing to be anything or nothing in the world's estimation, and publicly and privately, in season and out, avow their sympathy with despised and persecuted ideas and their advocates, and bear the consequences.

Her view of the abolitionist movement moved from one of a personal concern for the slave as a fellow human being to a political consciousness of the economic power that enforced slavery. She called for immediate and unconditional emancipation and helped found the Woman's National Loyal League, which demanded complete abolition of slavery through a thirteenth amendment.

Her longtime dearest friend Elizabeth Cady Stanton wrote, "In ancient Greece she would have been a Stoic; in the era of the Reformation a Calvinist; in King Charles's time a Puritan; but in the nineteenth century, by the very laws of her being, she is a reformer." Susan B. Anthony was a prophet in her own time, one who caught a vision of justice and invested her life in its realization. Like so many prophets before her, victory was denied during her lifetime. The Nineteenth Amendment was finally passed in 1920, a century after her birth. But the generation of women after Susan B. Anthony and

Elizabeth Cady Stanton did not share their view that political power was the key to better conditions for women. They sought rights, but without power analysis. Men had reduced rights to individuals, not classes. Anthony was a radical reformer. Merely liberal reform reduced social problems to individual ones, thereby masking the systemic causes of the problems themselves.

Susan B. Anthony, perhaps more than any other reformer of the nineteenth century, understood the nature of systemic change. There was little place for piety in her faith; prophecy was all. She fully understood how power works and how power is organized. By the age of fifty she was called the Napoleon of the women's movement, the most loved and hated woman in America. She stands as a singular exemplar of the prophetic imperative.

FRANCIS GREENWOOD PEABODY AND THE RISE OF THE SOCIAL GOSPEL

In his book, *The Rise of the Social Gospel,* Charles Howard Hopkins calls the Social Gospel "America's most unique contribution to the great ongoing stream of Christianity." He goes on to say,

This indigenous and typically American movement, initiated in the "gilded age," was called into being by the impact of modern industrial society and scientific thought upon the Protestantism of the United States during the half century following the Civil War. . . . The seedbed in which the ideological roots of social Christianity found themselves most at home was Unitarianism, which liberal faith was fundamentally ethical and intended to influence the conduct of life. It stressed the dignity and divine possibilities of man, the achievement of salvation through character culture, the unity and immanence of God, and the importance of the present life, and itself exerted a germinal influence upon other schools of American theology. The generous faith of Unitarianism in human nature, with its insistence upon humanitarian service, was illustrated by the inauguration in Boston in 1826 of a Unitarian "ministry at large" to the unchurched classes. This pioneer work, initiated and carried on for a number of years by the Reverend Joseph Tuckerman, was not only the first example of religious social service in America, but was also the first serious social effort on the part of a religious body to cope with the social and religious problems of the submerged population of a sizable city. . . as early as 1848 left wing Unitarian "religion of humanity" was distinctly hospitable to socialism.

Charles Howard Hopkins's words indicate that the Social Gospel was no foreign phenomenon foisted upon Unitarianism, but rather an integral part of it. This was true of Universalism as well, although it was perhaps not as influential as Unitarianism. From 1849 to 1863 the Universalist General Reform Association promoted the abolitionist struggle. The Association persuaded the General Convention of the Universalist Church to go on record in September 1855 as being utterly opposed to slavery. Although the Association died in the aftermath of the Civil War, Universalists began early to take an interest in the rights of labor, an emergent issue with the rise of a vigorous capitalism. G. H. Harmon of Tufts College called the attention of his fellow Universalists to the commercial and industrial abuses that led to an increase in poverty, suffering, and crime. *The Universalist Leader* devoted considerable editorial space to the discussion of labor problems, calling for labor justice through nonviolent means.

With the apparent resolution of the slavery question, the energies of the nation were turned to a broader Social Question, the problem of economic justice, the result of a rampant capitalism that created great gaps between rich and poor. The panics of 1873 and 1877 only served to underscore the urgency of the issue. It was not a new issue for Unitarians and Universalists, as we have seen, but it manifested itself in new ways. Karl Marx had written his searing critique of capitalism, and Americans were reading him in the light of their own situation. As Hopkins points out, Protestant Christians were not converted to socialism, much less to Marxism. In Unitarian circles there was a somewhat more receptive climate. The issue was not dissimilar to those raised earlier: did one change society through reform of the individual or must the whole social order be transformed? Initially, reformers tried to solve the problem of economic justice by applying the philanthropic principle of religion to contemporary issues without seriously modifying the old doctrines. They tried to bring about social justice by working on the personal religion of individuals, rather than on the systems in which they worked.

Into this situation stepped Francis Greenwood Peabody (1847–1936). Born in a Unitarian minister's home, he himself became minister of the church in Cambridge and in 1880 a professor at Harvard Divinity School. In 1883–1884 he introduced a course, "Ethical Theories and Social Problems: a practical examination of the questions of charity, temperance, labor, prisons, divorce, etc.," known to his students as "Peabo's drainage, drunkenness and divorce." Charles Howard Hopkins called him probably the first teacher of social ethics in the United States. He encouraged his mostly prosperous young students to take an active role in social welfare movements. He was an early promoter of what came to be called the Social Gospel.

In his *Jesus Christ and the Social Question* (1900), Peabody discussed the "Social Question" in terms of business methods, scientific discovery, and political forces. He found a contradiction between economic development and the social ideas of freedom and equality. The question was being raised in new and radical ways, for it was no longer a question of charity, but of justice. It was not enough to mitigate the evils of the existing order; one must question the very validity of that order. "Instead of generosity, men ask for justice; instead of alms, they demand work."

He attempted to reconcile the Christian church with social democracy. The church was seen by reformers as undergirding the status quo; this role must cease. By what means? Peabody rejected a return to early Christian communism as being irrelevant to industrial society. There is no one Christian economic order. Nor would Christian philanthropy any longer suffice; one must look to the causes of poverty.

He cited the "prophetic role" as a legitimate one for the Christian minister, who should be an advocate for righteousness, laying bare the sins of the people. The function of the prophet is not primarily to administer and organize, however, but to exhort and warn. What he advocated was not a Christian socialism, but a new examination of the social teachings of Jesus. In studying these teachings, he admitted that Jesus taught primarily a personal, face-to-face ethic; his teaching was episodic rather than systematic; it was a first-century agrarian teaching, not a twentieth-century industrial ethic. Yet the genius of Jesus's social teachings was that they did not propose specific remedies, but served to inspire people to seek out those remedies; Jesus stood above the social struggle and thus his teachings stood as an ideal, a judgment on every human enterprise; the end for Jesus was always to enrich spiritual life; the social life was but a means for its realization. The means was character, the end was love. Peabody realized that society influences people, but people also influence society, and the teachings of Jesus are to make good people who will make a just society.

When Peabody discussed the teaching of Jesus concerning the rich, he began to sound almost radical as he questioned whether there should be categories of rich and poor. "Is the possession of wealth on any terms justifiable?" He maintained that the institution of private property must be justified by its contribution to the public good. We must care for the poor. Yet does not charity do more harm than good? Is it not merely an anesthetic administered to the poor to keep them from fully comprehending their situation? We must go further than charity to examine the roots of the industrial order. What the poor need is not charity and temporary relief, but opportunity and power.

But then he retreated into a more pietistic mode when he cited the settlement house model of social reform, extolling the joy of patient service to a few discouraged souls. He criticized socialism for reducing all questions to the Social Question of the industrial order, although he admitted that it does affect every aspect of life. Still, the question was primarily spiritual: What sort of people will a given order produce?

Then, as if to illustrate his very real social ambivalence, he stepped very close to Marxism when he discussed the ideal industrial order, invoking the Marxist mantra, from each according to ability, to each according to need. Still, one cannot identify socialism with Jesus, for the Christian doctrine of the social order was so much more. Socialism began with economic needs and ended in economic change. Christianity began with spiritual needs and ended in the ideal of a spiritual kingdom.

Socialism sought to transform character by changing the economic order. Peabody believed that socialism might be religious, but religion was not socialism. These are parallel but not identical means. Again he moved away from a systemic interpretation of social change, concluding in the end that economic injustice exists not because the system is bad, but because people are. And so the socialist program became a kind of penalty the nation paid for refusing to apply the teachings of Jesus to the economic order. If the economic revolution comes, the old order must be replaced by one based on the teachings of Jesus; but if the teachings of Jesus were applied by the modern businessman, no revolution would be necessary. Peabody, then, stressed reconstituted character to deal with the Social Question, the humanization of industry, the conversion of business from an economic to a moral science. The role of the church in this Social Question was to be a spiritual powerhouse communicating power to change the people and thereby change the system.

What can we say of Peabody's relationship to the prophetic imperative? Clearly, he sensed a religious mandate to participate in history making. He defined the paths of religion as thought (rationalism), feeling (mysticism), and will (moral idealism). One of Peabody's contributions to the Social Gospel in Unitarian Universalism was seeking to spiritualize the Social Question and socialize religious life.

As to the corporate response of the church to this mandate, Peabody was unfortunately vague. The church clearly was much involved, but its corporate address was not much stressed. The settlement house approach (social service) was one vehicle; the prophetic voice of the pulpit (social witness) was another; Peabody's own work in teaching social ethics (social education) was clearly a third. However, he failed to develop an effective organizational response for social reform by the churches. The spirit was there, but the form was lacking.

Peabody's contribution to social analysis is ambiguous. As we have seen, he occasionally suggests a very radical critique of the capitalist system. He even employed language suggestive of Marxism at times. He raised the fundamental question of whether charity does more harm than good. Yet, just at the brink of systemic analysis, he retreated to preaching virtue to the business community. Instead of following through the implications of his questions as to why there are poverty and injustice and relating them to the social system that gave them birth, he was content to suggest that what is needed is simply better character. Still, Peabody must be seen as one who expanded the horizon of liberal religion in its acceptance of the Social Gospel. He clearly understood the difference between pietism and prophecy.

In his expansive discussion of the Social Question, then, Francis Greenwood Peabody set the stage for the Unitarian Universalist Social Gospel of the twentieth century. He was more a philosopher of that movement than its prophet, more a probing questioner of the social system than its reformer, but he did raise critical questions in a way that could not be ignored.

Twentieth-Century Reform

The advent of the twentieth century marked a turning point in liberal religious history in the area of social responsibility, as well as in denominational life in general. The nineteenth century had rushed to a close full of buoyant hope for the future. After all, Newton Mann (1836–1926) was the first minister to embrace the doctrine of evolution. The evolutionary view was applied to social progress by James Freeman Clarke (1810–1888), who in his succinct statement of Unitarian beliefs concluded with a ringing affirmation of faith in the "progress of Mankind onward and upward forever." However, new challenges were on the horizon: two world wars and an economic depression that would severely undercut this too easy optimism.

Universalists moved strongly toward the social gospel as the century dawned. Dr. Frank Oliver Hall preached successive sermons at Universalist General Convention gatherings on "The Gospel in an Age of Indifference" (1909) and "A Social Program for the Universalist Church" (1911). In his 1909 address he said that "the abject poverty of the many and the immeasurable wealth of the few is a disgrace not to the rich or the poverty-stricken individual necessarily, but to all of us who consent that such an unjust order of things should continue." And in 1911 he affirmed, "The Church must fight against conditions that make for ignorance and vice, poverty and disease, and for the establishment of others that insure health, happiness and prosperity." As a result, the convention appointed Hall chair of a Social Service Commission. In 1917 the Commission's secretary, Clarence R. Skinner, presented a Declaration of Social Principles and Social Programs, which was adopted by the General Convention. It included a rather radical statement on economic justice, advocating economic security for all. In 1919 a full-time social service secretary was employed to help implement these resolutions. Emerson Hugh Lalone wrote in his history of Universalist social action, "Generally speaking, however, throughout this post-war period the practical social idealism of our people was at a low ebb."

Clarence R. Skinner (1881–1949) was the social prophet of Universalism in this century. In 1914, at the age of thirty-three, Skinner was appointed to the chair of Applied Christianity at Crane Theological School (Universalist) at Tufts University. His short book *The Social Implications of Universalism*, which appeared in 1915, was compiled from his inaugural lecture series. Essentially, he transformed the theological principle of universal salvation into an ethical principle, ethical universalism, moving from the universal fatherhood of God to the universal brotherhood of man. He wrote, "The traditional Protestant Church is dying. . . . The individualism which called it into being is dying." He took issue with those who saw the path to social reform in the renewal of society by regenerating the individual. The individual was regenerated by the "progressive improvement of those conditions and environments which are within the social control and which largely determine character."

Skinner spoke from a prophetic imperative that saw the social dimensions of evil and the churches' corporate responsibility to deal with it. He has been faulted by subsequent critics, however, as naively optimistic. With many of the social gospelers, he failed to comprehend fully the nature of human self-interest and the nature of social power. Critic James Hunt writes:

> Certain questions should be raised concerning Skinner's theology and his ethics. When a faith becomes as closely identified with history as was the evolutionary social gospel, then that faith becomes vulnerable to history, especially when "the

great social and psychical movements of the twentieth century" (Skinner) turn out to include Nazism and Communism.

The Unitarian denomination began the new century with a flourish under the leadership of president Samuel A. Eliot (1862–1950). In
his 1904 presidential address he urged a corporate response to the
Social Question:

> Has not the time come when these free churches of ours, act-
> ing through their national Association, may enter more direct-
> ly and unitedly into tasks of education, of active charity, of
> social justice? . . . Unitarians as individuals have been the
> leaders of the American Commonwealth in all progressive
> reforms. Cannot the Unitarian body as a whole now assume
> that privilege of leadership which belongs to it by right of the
> labors and sacrifices of heroic men and women who have been
> trained in our principles?

In 1908 the American Unitarian Association accepted Eliot's recommendation for a Department of Social and Public Service. At that
same meeting, John Haynes Holmes, the newly settled young minister
of the Church of the Messiah in New York City, offered a statement of
social principles concerning public issues. He was opposed by the
Reverend Samuel M. Crothers, who said, "We are heartily in favor of
the spirit of this resolution, but we are in doubt as to anything introduced in a business meeting that seems to be a declaration of faith."
Holmes replied:

> It is time for the Unitarian Church to stop puttering with these
> questions of social reform and to put itself firmly on record as
> standing for something. . . . For a hundred years the Unitarian
> Church has led Christianity upon the side of theology, and I
> for one am dreaming of the day when the Unitarian Church of
> America shall lead the churches of this country upon the side
> of social reform.

The resolution proposed by Holmes was referred to the Unitarian
Commission on the Church and the Social Question and was never
acted on. The issue was joined. If Francis Greenwood Peabody was the
theoretician of the liberal religious social gospel, then John Haynes
Holmes (1879–1964) was its prophet. In May 1904 he had been
ordained and installed in the Third Religious Society of Dorchester,

Massachusetts, after his graduation from Harvard Divinity School. In his autobiography he recalls how the church and the Social Question came into consciousness as a central issue in his life.

"Like the Hebrew prophets of old, we must lift up our voices and spare not!" He believed the community had as much claim on him as did his church. And so, in 1909, the one-hundredth anniversary of Lincoln's birth, he helped organize the National Association for the Advancement of Colored People (NAACP). The year before he had helped establish the independent Unitarian Fellowship for Social Justice, which was to be a gadfly to the establishment for many years. During World War I he became a charter member of the pacifist Fellowship of Reconciliation, and he helped establish what later became the American Civil Liberties Union.

World War I heightened the tension between the radicals and the establishment of the denomination. While President Wilson urged neutrality, Unitarians began to side with England, and the American Unitarian Association (AUA) asked support of the War Distress Fund. Holmes, minister of what is now the Community Church of New York, responded with nine consecutive sermons on force versus nonresistance, in which he advocated a pacifist position. Although his own board of trustees disagreed with him unanimously, they pledged to support his freedom of the pulpit, and both board and congregation refused to accept his proffered resignation over the issue.

The denomination was not so tolerant. President Wilson's move from neutrality to active participation in the war set the stage for controversy. At the 1917 General Conference in Montreal, former president William Howard Taft, moderator of the meeting, exhorted the delegates "to . . . express [their] emphatic approval of all that President Wilson and Congress have done and are doing to win this war."

Holmes argued passionately against this resolution, but it was adopted by a vote of 236 to 9. In the following year the AUA, concerned that certain ministers were causing discord in their parishes by continued opposition to the war, invoked sanctions, declaring that "any society which employs a minister who is not a willing, earnest and outspoken supporter of the United States in the vigorous and resolute prosecution of the war cannot be considered eligible for aid from the Association."

Holmes responded by withdrawing from the fellowship of Unitarian ministers. At the same time his church left the denomination. Holmes then launched a community church movement with his own church in the forefront. He drafted a statement of purpose for the new church:

The Community Church is an institution of religion dedicated to the service of humanity. It is distinctive from other churches in these points: . . . It substitutes for loyalty to the single denomination, loyalty to the social group. Its first affiliation is not with any denomination, but with the community as a whole. It substitutes for a private group of persons held together by common theological beliefs or viewpoints, the public group of citizens held together by common social interests. . . . It substitutes for the individual the social group as an object of salvation. It interprets religion in terms of social reconstruction, and dedicates its members to the fulfillment of social idealism. . . . The core of its faith, as the purpose of its life, is the Beloved Community.

Holmes remained active in causes after the war. He was a leading supporter of Margaret Sanger and her planned parenthood movement, and with Drs. Hannah and Abraham Stone he founded in his own church a Marriage Consultation Clinic. From 1920 to 1927 he was a leading supporter of Sacco and Vanzetti. He also encouraged the progressive movement of Robert LaFollette, for the only time in his career taking an active part in a partisan political campaign. He later joined the Socialist Party and preached the memorial service for its founder, Eugene Debs.

At the time of World War II, Holmes once again affirmed his pacifism and once again offered his resignation. As before, his congregation, whom he had served for over thirty-five years, refused to accept it. For his long ministry he was awarded the Sixth Annual Unitarian Award in 1954 for distinguished service to the cause of liberal religion. The very denomination that had spurned him for his radical stance now embraced him.

What are the contributions of John Haynes Holmes to the prophetic imperative? He definitely saw himself as a social prophet and the church as a prophetic church. His somewhat grandiloquent style suggests this: "Rather will it [the church] come to be regarded as an armory whence the soldiers of God shall march forth to battle against the legions of Satan."

He discerned that for individuals to be saved, the society must be saved: "The church will care . . . not so much for emancipating men from what we call sin, as for emancipating them from the conditions of life and labor which make sin inevitable; not so much for saving souls, as for saving the society which molds the soul for eternal good or ill."

His systemic analysis of the causes of social injustice clearly places him within the prophetic imperative, as does his understanding of the church as corporate agent. It provided support for him and the voluntary associations in which he participated, and it took corporate stands at critical times. For example, Holmes once read a stirring resolution calling for an investigation of New York mayor Jimmy Walker: "we, the congregation of the Community Church, and citizens of New York, . . . do call upon the Governor of New York and Mayor of the City of New York . . . to use their every power . . . to expose wickedness in high places. . . ." After Holmes had read the resolution, the congregation rose to their feet in prolonged applause and then bowed their heads in benediction.

And yet, as his biographer Carl Hermann Voss points out,

> He had a simplistic approach to problems both individual and social and was often naive about men's motives, seemingly unaware of the extent of evil in the world and confident that moral suasion would alter an inequitable society. . . . He underestimated the class struggle and retained illusions about the possibility of dislodging deeply entrenched interests of power. He seemed unaware of the collective egoism of social organisms and appeared not to discern the close tie between conduct and interest in both individual and society.

Nevertheless, Holmes stands as one of the liberal religious prophets of the twentieth century, one who spoke from a prophetic pulpit and carried that message into the controversies of his time. He was not content with the social education of his sermons and speeches; not content with social service as an antidote to economic injustice, not even content with his witness from pulpit and in the streets. He advocated a corporate social action not only by his Community Church, but by the several voluntary associations he helped found.

The citation to Holmes in the denomination's distinguished service award included these words: "A leading exponent of the social gospel, he has both preached and practiced it tirelessly through the years." When we look at those years of ministry, from 1904 through 1949, a period of war, racism, economic depression, and social upheaval, it is clear that Holmes made a strong contribution to the prophetic imperative of liberal religion.

James Luther Adams and the Voluntary Association

In James Luther Adams (1901–1994) we find a figure who combines the careful scholarship of Francis Greenwood Peabody, who was a powerful influence upon him, and the prophetic zeal of John Haynes Holmes, a colleague for many years. Adams was born of fundamentalist parents; his father was a Baptist country preacher. He rebelled against this background into a rational scientific humanism in his college and seminary days, encountered Christian realism, and synthesized all these into a prophetic liberal Christianity.

His career was one of wide-ranging teaching in theological schools at Harvard, the University of Chicago, Meadville/Lombard, and Andover Newton, as well as countless other seminaries and universities around the world. In his teaching as in his citizenship, Adams embraced the prophetic imperative. "The holy thing," he wrote, "is the participation in those processes that give body and form to universal justice."

His social responsibility involvements were many. In 1942 he was a founder and later chairman of the Independent Voters of Illinois, organized to defeat isolationist sentiment in the Midwest. Adams had been chastened by the writings of Reinhold Niebuhr. His several visits to Nazi Germany in the thirties persuaded him that Hitler was demonic and must be opposed, even through war. He was active in the American Civil Liberties Union, in reforming the Chicago public schools, and in working for desegregation in many institutions over the years. Adams was an active churchman. He poured himself into the labor–management dispute in Salem, Massachusetts, his first parish, although members of opposing factions were also members of his church. At the denominational level he was an influential figure in organizing for social action. As one of the authors of the Report of the Study Commission in 1936, *Unitarians Face a New Age*, he urged a new thrust in denominational social action. In a section on the mandate before the churches, the report concluded:

> These churches will affirm their belief that religion is futile and sterile unless it has direct and effective bearing upon the problems of human society. They will be unsparing in their criticism of the evils and injustice now existing in the world, and they will work unceasingly for a better social order. . . . They will consider it a part of their business to make available accurate and reliable information on social conditions, and they will not hesitate to take appropriate action in times of social emergency or stress, remembering always that in their action they must remain loyal to faith in education as the primary method of democracy. In the present conflict of social forces they will throw the weight of their influence on the side

of every agency which seeks to promote human welfare by methods consistent with their religion.

In underscoring the centrality of the prophetic imperative to Unitarianism, the report stated:

> No part of the Unitarian tradition is clearer than that which affirms the necessary relations between religion and social action, and the record of the denomination in the field of service for social reform and the advancement of social justice must not be jeopardized now. On this point it would be a calamity to waver, or to give any appearance of wavering.

In this report the Commission suggested a threefold division of the denomination's social thrust: (1) Social education on public issues would be vested in the department of education "at the very center of our most important departments where this work would naturally serve as the nucleus for the entire program of the bureau;" (2) the representative function (social witness), participation in various interfaith groups, for example, would be a responsibility of the American Unitarian Association Board of Trustees; and (3) the prophetic or more radical thrust (social action) would be entrusted to the existing Unitarian Fellowship for Social Justice (UFSJ), which would be given more denominational support, although it would remain an autonomous body. This group would serve as a gadfly to the movement.

Adams himself became both theoretician and practitioner of the church as a voluntary association. While this contribution will be discussed later in this study, the essential point for present purposes is the "pragmatic theory of meaning." That is, any belief that effectively exists in history must have form, and the creation of this form requires institutional power. Here is the theological basis for Adams's associational theory of history. In his view, history is powerfully shaped by voluntary groupings of people seeking common goals. Society is not transformed by mere change in attitude, but by the mobilization of social power. So important is participation in these voluntary associations that Adams has paraphrased the biblical comment to read "By their groups ye shall know them."

Adams fully recognized that the great problem in our day is one more of collective sin than private sin. It is difficult to identify guilt and responsibility in a mass society where "nobody did it," although we recognize the machinations of the great social forces: the state, the commercial powers, the labor unions, the voluntary associations, and the rest. Adams believed that the most dangerous power now is not government, over which we have some democratic control, but the large business institutions, over which we have little control. He expanded on Lord Acton's dictum that "power tends to corrupt and absolute power corrupts absolutely" to say that "Impotence tends to corrupt. Absolute impotence corrupts absolutely." Throughout his career he urged voluntary associations, including church groups, to learn to use their power to promote social justice. The title of his address at the inaugural convocation of the Boston Theological Institute suggests that mandate: "Blessed Are the Powerful." Here he advocates responsible use of ecclesiastical power.

Of critical importance to this study is his ardent involvement in the life of the church. His participation in the 1936 study commission, his role in the creation of a denominational Department of Social Responsibility, whose advisory committee he chaired, his active involvement as a layman in churches he joined, all testify to the importance of the corporate role of the church in the quest for social justice.

In response to a layman's query as to whether voting resolutions on matters of public policy by religious institutions constituted a violation of the principle of separation of church and state, Adams wrote an essay entitled "On Interference." He justified such action on the basis of three criteria: "The church as a corporate body, I would say, should in its witness intend to be visible, to be credible and to be accountable."

He went on to elaborate on the three by saying that invisibility of the churches on matters of public policy is interpreted as a sign of neutrality, of indifference. He cited the issue of slavery to indicate that corporate silence was interpreted as indifference on that great moral question. Churches need to be credible by making an effort to vindicate the claim they make. He lamented the lack of guidelines provided by the church in current scandals involving multinational corporations. The churches must be accountable, they must come under the judgment of the community in which they live, "which in turn comes under the Judgment of God. They are accountable for the performance or nonperformance of their religious–ethical witness. . . ."

James Luther Adams has been the most articulate embodiment of the Unitarian Universalist prophetic imperative in our time. His career was one of social education, through his extensive teaching, speaking, and writing. Social service was part of his work at Gould Farm in Massachusetts, an intentional community. His social witness was made many times in articles, demonstrations, and speeches. His social action stance is suggested by his active involvement in numerous groups, religious and secular, that sought systemic social change.

THE PROPHETIC IMPERATIVE TODAY

The Benevolent Fraternity of Unitarian Churches is the oldest social action program supported by religious liberals. It began as a ministry to the poor, and while it still emphasizes a direct-services approach to students, mental patients, and the elderly, it is moving into a more corporate and systemic stance. Now renamed the Unitarian Universalist Urban Ministry, it is described as follows in the UUA *Directory:*

> An alliance for urban ministry of 56 Unitarian Universalist societies that has provided ministry-at-large to the poor of Boston since 1834. Programs include: Renewal House, a program for women and children in crisis; Refugee and Immigrant Women's Outreach; and First Church in Roxbury Youth Programs and Community Center. The UU Urban Ministry sponsors the Tuckerman Coalition, a statewide coalition of clergy and lay leaders involved with public policy.

The Vietnam War energized Unitarian Universalists as have few other events in American history. While the majority of ministers and laypeople seemed to oppose the war, a significant minority supported it. Congregations were split over the war, sanctuary for draft resisters, and the proposed amnesty following. Several denominational resolutions condemned U.S. policy, and Unitarian Universalists were among antiwar protesters at local and national demonstrations. Unitarian Universalist layman Michael Ferber was one of the Boston Four who led a ceremony of draft-card burning at the Arlington Street Church in Boston in the late sixties. A controversial Unitarian Universalist Service Committee project in Vietnam was terminated because of protest. Perhaps most dramatic was the UUA-affiliated Beacon Press publication of Senator Mike Gravel's *Pentagon Papers* revealing administration duplicity in Vietnam. The federal government subpoenaed contribution lists from UUA headquarters, but President Robert West and the board of trustees took the matter to court. The government later dropped the action.

One of the most painful chapters in recent social justice history was the denominational struggle against racism. While Unitarians and Universalists have long prided themselves on their actions for racial justice, the advent of the Black Power movement during the most torturous period of the civil rights revolution challenged the liberal integrationist philosophy that had prevailed for years. That phase culminated in the 1965 Selma campaign during which the Reverend

James Reeb, a Unitarian Universalist minister, was killed by white men on the streets of Selma, Alabama. The denomination's board of trustees adjourned its meeting from Boston to Selma for the memorial service. UUA support of Martin Luther King, Jr.'s nonviolent campaigns marked the high point of liberal religious involvement.

In the wake of the call for Black Power, a controversial Black Affairs Council (BAC) was created by the 1968 Unitarian Universalist Association General Assembly in Cleveland as a nonprofit funding and program agency to seek systemic change to benefit African Americans. It had three components: Community Organization, Economic Development, and Political Education; it was designed to support and fund programs within the black community that led to empowerment, unification, and self-determination. After a tumultuous debate the General Assembly delegates pledged $1 million to BAC over a four-year period.

Black and White Action (BAWA) emerged as an integrationist response to BAC and followed the more traditional race relations pattern of the civil rights movement. It was primarily engaged in educational and cultural programs to celebrate ethnic diversity, although it also supported community-oriented action programs consistent with its approach.

The issue was joined again at the UUA's 1969 General Assembly in Boston. As denominational resources dwindled and racial controversy deepened, the denomination's board of trustees stated that it could not fully fund BAC, whereupon several hundred delegates left the assembly floor to reconvene in the sanctuary of the Arlington Street Church. After arduous negotiations, a compromise was reached, but BAC eventually fell victim to lack of funding and unresolved racial justice philosophy among Unitarian Universalists. The whole BAC–BAWA controversy demonstrates the capacity of people of good will to agree to disagree, albeit sometimes disagreeably. (For a detailed narrative and varying interpretations, read *Unitarian Universalism and the Quest for Racial Justice* by the UUA Commission on Appraisal, and *The Black Empowerment Controversy and the UUA* by Victor Carpenter. For a more comprehensive historical study of race and racism in the movement, see Mark Morrison-Reed's *Black Pioneers in a White Denomination*. See the bibliography for details.) More recently, the denomination has made creation of nonracist, multicultural communities its focus in a Journey Toward Wholeness program, which focuses on white institutional racism. This approach has been challenged by African American theologian Thandeka, who suggests the issue is at least as much a matter of class as of race. In *Learning to Be White*, she questions whether our positive view of human nature is compatible with the inherent assumption of racism in white people implied by the program. The debate rages on.

This brief history of the Unitarian Universalist Association suggests how far the movement has come toward a corporate address to systemic change. A 1985 study commission chaired by UUA President John Buehrens (1993–2001) concluded that the Faith in Action: A UUA Department for Diversity and Justice (its current name) should focus its primary energies on empowering local congregations to act in their own communities. Thus, training activists is the central thrust for the department. Several programs have evolved, including antiracism training; the Jubilee Working Group for Anti-Racism; Journey Toward Wholeness Sunday; Social Justice Programs; The Washington Office; the Office of Bisexual, Gay, Lesbian, and Transgender Concerns; Anti-Oppression Education and Resources; and Accessibility Advocacy. The Commission on Social Witness facilitates the process by which General Resolutions are prepared, adopted, and implemented by the UUA and its member societies. These statements of social witness provide guidance for UUA staff members and local congregations. The UUA has developed a moral audit of its investments and has used its holdings to present social issues at corporate stockholder meetings.

The Unitarian Universalist United Nations Office, formerly a part of the denominational structure, works as an affiliate group to involve the movement in international affairs. The Unitarian Universalist Women's Federation, another affiliate group, has worked on legislation for women's rights, including support of the Equal Rights Amendment. The Unitarian Universalist Peace Fellowship continues its witness for peace. More recently, other groups have become affiliate groups within the Unitarian Universalist family: Unitarian Universalists for a Just Economic Community, the Seventh Principle Project (working in the field of eco-justice), a battered women's support network, an animal rights group, Unitarian Universalists against the Death Penalty, and many more that are listed in the annual directory of the Association. The Holdeen Fund has made possible extensive work in India, focusing on the economic empowerment of women. The Unitarian Universalist Funding Program, supported by grants from the Veatch Program of the Unitarian Universalist Congregation at Shelter Rock, Long Island, makes grants to social justice groups.

The Unitarian Universalist Funding Program has two panels devoted to social action: the Fund for a Just Society makes grants to community-based social action programs, and the Fund for Unitarian

Universalist Social Responsibility assists specifically Unitarian Universalist action projects. (For further information write the UU Funding Program, P. O. Box 40, Boston, MA, 02117.) The Veatch Program itself has invested millions of dollars in social justice work across the country.

Most instructive, however, would be a brief look at the Unitarian Universalist Service Committee (UUSC), which is perhaps the clearest example of the prophetic imperative in contemporary Unitarian Universalism. It is by far the largest social justice program in the movement. Incorporated as the Unitarian Service Committee in 1939 and the Universalist Service Committee in 1945, the two denominational agencies merged in 1963 after the consolidation of the American Unitarian Association and the Universalist Church of America in 1961. Both agencies began with a direct ministry to political and other refugees of war.

A second stage of development is seen in the emphasis of the Unitarian Universalist Service Committee on demonstration projects at home and abroad. Specialists in health care, social work, and technical assistance were funded to develop what would become self-sustaining projects staffed by indigenous people. Subsequently, the committee moved on to other projects. This pattern still describes part of its program. In Haiti, for example, a planned parenthood program, initially opposed by the government, evolved into a comprehensive community development program that is now part of national policy. It has served as a model for other Caribbean and several African nations. The Service Committee has mobilized the talents and resources of Unitarian Universalists around the country to press for reform and social change and service. Abroad, the Service Committee joins with nationals in host countries to effect democratic change and social justice.

A third stage in development of a UUSC philosophy and program is the empowerment of powerless peoples. Building on the *concientizacao* (consciousness-raising) techniques of Paulo Freire in *The Pedagogy of the Oppressed,* UUSC seeks "to counter the ignorance and passivity of the very poor, a combination deadening people's abilities to analyze and change their living conditions. Projects in Central and Latin America, Africa and India promote social justice by teaching the economic, social and political facts of life as the necessary first steps to changing these conditions."

In the eighties a major program was the National Moratorium on Prison Construction, in cooperation with the National Council on Crime and Delinquency. Here the focus was not on direct ministry to the imprisoned, but an attempt through social education, witness, and action to effect a ten-year moratorium on all prison construction in the United States, thus forcing a critical examination of alternatives to incarceration. This goal was sought through lobbying at state and federal levels, but the program was finally terminated.

In the nineties the focus of domestic programs was the Promise the Children program, which combines action at local, state, and federal levels as advocates for children through service, education, witness, and legislation. A Washington office provides access to the political levers of power on both domestic and international issues. More recently, UUSC has created the Just Works program as a vehicle for involving Unitarian Universalist volunteers in social justice work. In the wake of federal welfare reform in 1996, UUSC developed a comprehensive evaluation program to point out weaknesses in the program and call for more radical reform. *Roots and Vision* by Ghanda Di Figlia details the first fifty years of the Service Committee's efforts in social change.

In the work of the UUSC we see clearly the long road from the very modest ministry to the poor in Boston to an extensive effort of religiously based corporate advocacy designed to affect the institutional structures of society. While social education, social service, and social witness are encompassed in this work, the key to both UUA and UUSC programs is social action, the corporate address of the church to the systemic problems of the society in which it lives.

Summary

The prophetic imperative had its beginnings in ancient Israel and was made manifest in the prophet Jesus and the early church. In the *Book of Acts* we read that the early Christians were those "who have turned the world upside down." Our liberal religious tradition traces its roots to the radical reformation of the sixteenth century, the Anabaptists. This heretical band was a creative minority in resisting war and injustice. But part of our tradition is also Calvinist—that group against which our forebears rebelled. We left, but took something of value with us.

The Calvinists, who in their zeal martyred our own Michael Servetus, were the first self-disciplined agents of social and political reconstruction in Western history. Previously, people saw their religious function as adapting to whatever history presented them. With John Calvin and his followers, we have a group who believed that history could be transformed into the Kingdom of God.

An illustration of this comes from a fascinating study of religious social reform. It was noted at the St. Bavo Kerk in Haarlem, the Netherlands, that the Calvinists had put representations of good solid Dutch burghers in the windows where medieval Catholics would have had saints. Only then came the realization that these were the Calvinist saints. They had not retreated into some monastery to contemplate the world; they had remained in their communities to change it.

Channing claimed that religion is a social principle. Now, over a century and a half later, this social principle has taken on institutional form. While it is still uttered from the pulpit and taught in the classroom, it has moved into the structural relations of the church and society. It has been chastened with the too easy optimism of the early Social Gospel period. It has become more sophisticated with respect to the depths of human nature and the complexity of social change. The Beloved Community is not yet at hand, nor is it around the corner. The quest for the Beloved Community is a long and disciplined process of responding to the prophetic imperative. This process is one in which individuals of good will associate themselves in disciplined groups to transform the structures that shape human lives. This is the wind Unitarian Universalists have inherited. It is a disquieting wind, and it remains to be seen whether it is deserved.

CHAPTER FOUR

Harnessing Our
Deepest Explosions

Former Yale chaplain and religious activist William Sloan Coffin is reputed to have said, "Unitarian Universalists have such a thick ethic and such a thin theology." I suppose he meant that, while we are mightily engaged in the ethical issues of our day, we lack a robust theological rationale for our action. It is possible that Coffin is right, for Unitarian Universalists do better dealing with the *how* of acting on social problems than with the *why* of confronting them in the first place. Theology has to do with the whys of human existence—in the present context the whys of social action. James Luther Adams reminded us that right attitudes are never enough for social justice; they must be embodied in social institutions. This is what Adams called a "pragmatic theory of meaning." Such a theory implies that a theology needs social expression and that social responsibility needs a theological base. We must have a theology to undergird the prophetic imperative. My approach is that of confessional theology: articulating my faith as best I can without apology and without intent to convert another to my point of view. While a number of theologies of social action are available to the Unitarian Universalist, my own theological rationale for social responsibility is grounded in a mystical religious humanism.

FUNCTIONAL ULTIMACY AND AUTHORITY IN RELIGION

William Jones, professor of religion and director of black studies at Florida State University, in his book *Is God a White Racist?* provides a humanist theological stance that he calls *functional ultimacy*. He goes on to say that we human beings are the ultimate seat of authority not because we are omniscient, but simply because our human nature equips us with "permanent sunglasses which we cannot remove." Our decisions are analogous to a decree of the Supreme Court, ultimate and final because they are unappealable. However, the Court is only the "final interpreter of the Constitution, not its creator."

We live in objective uncertainty, never absolutely sure that what we have found at any given time is the final truth. Take the story of Abraham and Isaac in the Hebrew scriptures. Abraham has been commanded, presumably by Yahweh, to take his beloved son Isaac into the wilderness and slay him as a sacrifice. At the last moment a voice intervenes to tell Abraham to stay his hand. How does Abraham know if the voice is that of Yahweh or of Moloch, the Canaanite god of fire to whom children were offered in sacrifice? He is thrown back on his own subjectivity and must live in objective uncertainty. Abraham must assume the mantle of ultimate valuator, of final arbiter. He must decide the source of the command, and in making this judgment he determines the value of the command. If he concludes that the decree is from Yahweh, it is morally imperative. If, however, he decides that the voice is Moloch's, the order must be rejected. But clearly, only Abraham can make this decision.

So we are functionally ultimate in that we must make choices out of our own concept of truth and goodness. We are actors in the drama of life, but not its director. We must in the end make a decision, fraught with subjectivity, regarding the truth claims we make. This is not the same as saying we are omnicompetent or omnipotent. We live in a reality greater than ourselves; as finite creatures we make sense of it as best we can. We are the measurer, not the measure; the creature, not the creator, of all things. Functional ultimacy, then, is the point of departure, not termination.

In the last analysis, any decision we make constitutes a wager. We make a decision based on truth as we understand it, although we cannot demonstrate the truth of our choice. In short, we are caught in what Jones calls the "humanocentric predicament" in which we cannot shed our human nature.

The individual, then, is a co-creator of freedom, authority and value. No one can make absolute truth claims, for each of us is limited by our own circumscribed perspective. We engage in the quest for truth as coequals, able to criticize one another, to test alternatives, and to choose on the basis of the increased insight. Hence, a community is critical to the process of decision making. The use of freedom, reason, and tolerance is a central feature of the liberal religious community that has consistently rejected special revelation. Truth claims must be open to criticism by people as coequal centers of choosing. The story of religious history can be seen in part as the struggle between truth claims based on divine revelation and those based on community consensus. Each new conceptualization of truth is in turn succeeded by subsequent communities of thought so that the process by which truth is defined becomes central. The ideal here is not the Lone Ranger, the solitary individual, but a community of the dialogue that presupposes the democratic process in our congregations and in society at large.

Therefore, the prophetic church is mandated to a dialogic process regarding competing theological, ethical, and social claims. The process presupposes a creedless church as a context for building a theology. This, however, is not enough, for theology is always particular, asserting certain assumptions about its specific world-view. In Unitarian Universalism these assumptions do not rest on a specific event, person, or literature as the norm. There is a tradition in liberal religion, but it cannot claim as central and normative a place as in the revealed religions of the biblical tradition, for example. Unitarian Universalism, therefore, is not committed to a saving event or person, but to a process—an ongoing quest for religious meaning.

Feminist theologian Sharon Welch in *A Feminist Ethic of Risk* maintains that the community is the core of ethics in that "a single actor cannot be moral." This is an arrogance that fails to recognize that all perspectives are partial and that the creation of a moral vision requires the counterbalance of other people and groups. "[P]luralism," she contends, "is required, not for its own sake, but for the sake of enlarging our moral vision" and "is grounded in moral dialogue and openness to political conflict" and "requires dialogue with actual members of different communities."

The communal nature of our theological method is aptly summarized in the African proverb, "I am because we are." Again, the African epigram "It takes a whole village to raise a child" suggests that it takes a whole religious community to build a theology of social responsibility.

THEOLOGICAL ASSUMPTIONS FOR SOCIAL RESPONSIBILITY

In the absence of a creedal or doctrinal tradition focusing on the content of specific beliefs, the Unitarian Universalist social ethicist is prompted to use theological resources as they emerge from personal experience and interaction with the community. This is not to say one must invent the wheel theologically; there is a tradition of theologizing, but the emphasis historically has been, first, a heretical stance usually to the left of mainline Christianity and, more recently, an emphasis on the process by which religious values are developed and the stories of this development. The religious community provides the personal and social setting in which theologizing is done, but the basic responsibility rests with the individual. Hence, any theological assumptions for liberal religion must be drawn at the personal level, but shared in the communal dialogue. My own theological model understands our task as creating and maintaining relationships between the self and the realities that we encounter. In the final analysis, it is practical in purpose. As the nineteenth-century Universalist theologian Hosea Ballou put it, "There is one inevitable criterion of judgment touching religious faith in doctrinal matters: can you reduce it to practice? If not, have none of it."

Religion I take to be that core of ultimate meanings, values, and convictions to which we commit our lives. Meanings are the whys of human behavior, the purposes that explain our behavior, those reflections on values within an ultimate frame of reference and which in turn inform those values. Values are those guidelines by which we understand the world and act upon it, the internal directives that determine the direction of one's life story. Convictions are the living out of these meanings and values in action; they drive behavior. For example, the natural world is a source of intense enjoyment and great meaning for me; I value the world as sacred—nature has inherent rights to preservation; therefore, I act out of an eco-justice ethic to be a responsible trustee of that natural world.

Religion, then, is more than beliefs, which are intellectual constructs. Meanings, values, and convictions are existential constructs, intellectual, affectional and operational. Theology is the articulation of, reflection on, and criticism of these values, meanings, and convictions in that ultimate context. It involves looking at the self from a cosmic perspective or, more theologically put, getting what religious educator Angus H. MacLean called a "God's-eye-view of the self."

The mature religious person is continually engaged in a variety of life tasks that address certain fundamental problems, the solutions to which are crucial to religious functioning. Each of these tasks is addressed on a continuing basis throughout life.

My theological model has its roots in anthropology; that is, it is rooted in human experience, the result of the tough and tender experiences of life. It emerged from people who tried to make some sense out of the world in which they lived. Theology, then, begins with the self—the first bit of raw data that we encounter as theologians. Hence, our understanding of human nature becomes determinative for our theologizing. The self has transactions with ultimate reality, with historical reality, with social reality, and with the reality of its own depth—call it soul, if you will. Out of these transactions emerge values

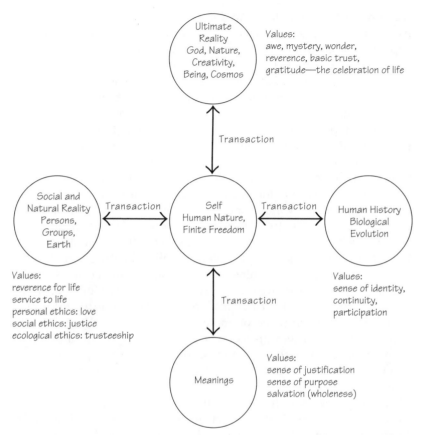

A Theological Model

and meanings I call religious. The model shown above is a graphic representation of this understanding.

Human Nature

If we are the measurers of all things theological, we clearly need to know something about ourselves—the issue is human nature. Traditionally, Unitarian Universalists have held a very optimistic view of human nature, what Roman Catholic creation theologian Matthew Fox calls "original blessedness," as opposed to the traditional orthodox Christian doctrine of original sin. We have understood that human beings are rational creatures, creatures of evolution. We have not paid nearly as much attention to our capacity for sin, a concept about which we don't much like to talk. We don't do very well explaining human nature, for example, in terms of the Holocaust, nor can we adequately explain that the best and the brightest brought the world the Vietnam War. We don't really have a tragic sense of life.

We are enamored of the sanctity of the separate individual, faith in a preestablished historical harmony, and we tend to entertain overly rational and optimistic perspectives on human nature and the inevitability of progress with a view to the ultimate perfectibility of society. In 1885 this liberal confidence in human nature was given classic expression in "Five Points," James Freeman Clark's response to Calvinism described by David Robinson in *The Unitarians and the Universalists*. The last point affirmed faith in "[t]he *Continuity of Human Development* in all worlds, or the *Progress of Mankind* onward and upward forever." The 1936 Universalist Avowal of Faith unequivocally stated belief "in the power of men of good will and sacrificial spirit to overcome all evil and progressively establish the Kingdom of God." In the 1967 Goals Survey, nine in ten Unitarian Universalists agreed that our "potential for love can overcome our potential for evil." In the 1985 "Purposes and Principles" of the Unitarian Universalist Association "we affirm and promote . . . the goal of world community with peace, liberty and justice for all." Unitarian Universalists have been irrepressibly optimistic, almost to a fault. But, if people are so good by nature, why in the world does humanity so often seem to be in such a mess?

Arrayed against this optimistic view is the more traditional Christian view of original sin as articulated in Reinhold Niebuhr's *The Nature and Destiny of Man* and *The Children of Light and the Children of Darkness*. It holds we are willful, even arrogant creatures. Niebuhr said, "Sin is the most easily documented of all human traits, witness the blood-soaked path of human history." He once suggested that each person secretly thinks he or she is the "end-product of evolution— what God was really trying to accomplish all this time." Applying this to the social order, Niebuhr concluded that "Man's capacity for justice makes democracy possible; but man's inclination to injustice makes democracy necessary."

The inevitable humility we experience in the face of the evidence was colorfully put some time ago by an unknown writer: "What are we when you come to think of us, but minutely set, ingenious machines for turning, with infinite artfulness, the red wine of Shiraz into urine?" Or, as anthropologist Ashley Montague put it, "At last we have discovered the missing link between our anthropoid ancestors and truly civilized [beings]—us."

We do need to take sin seriously, but in the Old Testament sense—missing the mark—as an archer seeks to hit the bull's-eye and only occasionally succeeds. I conclude, then, that human nature is best described by theologian Paul Tillich's phrase "finite freedom." Or to use James Luther Adams's formulation, "We are both fated and free." Human nature exists in a tension between the will to mutuality and the will to power. Our will is ambiguous. While we have the potential to transcend ourselves, we can also be utterly selfish. Our potential for creativity is matched by our propensity for destruction. While we are temples of the spirit, we are also houses of flesh and blood. The line between good and evil runs right through the middle of each human heart.

We continue to exist in the tension between self-love, in Niebuhr's sense of pretension, arrogance, overreaching, and the thought of psychologist Carl Rogers, who felt that the basic human problem was that people have too little self-regard. He believed that self-love was needed to become fully human beings. Our paradoxical nature is summed up in Viktor Frankl's vivid description of his concentration camp experience in *Man's Search for Meaning:* "Man could be defined as the being who invented the gas chambers for human extermination. But man can also be defined as the being who entered those gas chambers with the stirring tune of the 'Marseilles,' or the Lord's Prayer on his lips."

Ultimate Reality

The self has transactions with a reality that may be variously described, scientifically, poetically, and theologically, as ultimate reality, cosmos, nature, being, God, or creativity (see Henry Nelson Wieman's *The Source of Human Good*). A primary task of the religious person is to come to terms with our relationship to that sustaining reality in which we live, move, and have our being. The transaction between the self and ultimate reality precipitates human values—awe, reverence, mystery, wonder, basic trust in being, gratitude—and gives rise to worship (the celebration of life) and ethics (the service of life). This is part of the depth dimension of human experience.

People exist in a cosmic setting; we have a cosmic connection with the ground of being or ultimate reality. Human nature has its ultimate context. Religion emerges in part out of the relationship of self and cosmos. We live in both a spiritual and physical environment. The point at which we touch is our own creation, for we are integral parts of this cosmic creativity—cocreators with it. Traditionally, this cosmic setting has been called God, and there are many Unitarian Universalists who prefer to use that term in theologizing.

A 1987 survey by the Unitarian Universalist Association provided an overview of theological positions regarding the God concept.

Which of the following statements comes closest to expressing your beliefs about God?

- God is a supernatural being who reveals himself in human experience and history.   4%
- God is the ground of all being, real but not adequately describable.   28%
- God may appropriately be used as a name for some natural processes within the universe, such as love or creative evolution.   49%
- God is an irrelevant concept, and the central focus of religion should be on man's knowledge and values.   18%
- God is a concept that is harmful to a worthwhile religion.   2%

This update of a 1967 survey added a new question: "The way I would describe the divine for myself is. . . . "

- creative force   29%
- highest potential   18%
- harmony with nature   11%
- unknowable power   11%
- uncertain   11%
- superior being   3%
- meaningless   3%
- harmful concept   14%

The Unitarian Universalist *Fulfilling the Promise* program in 1998 listed the following theological categories with the preference percentage.

- Humanist   46.1%
- Earth/nature centered   19%
- Theist   13%
- Christian   9.5%
- Mystic   6.2%
- Buddhist   3.6%

- Jewish   1.3%
- Hindu   0.4%
- Moslem   0.1%
- Other   13.3%

The question of the nature of God or ultimate reality is an open one for us. We know that we are part of a cosmic reality greater than ourselves, but we are hard put to name it. Some believe that to name it is to diminish it. I am less concerned with answering that metaphysical question and more concerned that religious liberals have experiences of this reality that move us to action. I prefer to share my experience of the sacred, rather than to speculate about the existence of a divine being.

It may be that the most valuable function of liberal religious theology is asking the right questions about ultimate reality: Is it benign? Does it have a will of its own? Does it intervene in human affairs? Does it make any difference in our lives? We may not succeed in answering all of our questions. The provisional answers that we have found may only serve to raise a whole set of new questions. In some ways we may feel as confused as ever, but perhaps we will be confused on a higher level and about more important things.

It may be, for instance, that God is best understood not as a noun, but as a verb. That is, the word may not refer to any being up there or out there or even in there, but to a divine process of which we are part. It may be that we experience the sacred in relational power—that it is created out of the gathering of people in worship or in pursuit of a noble cause. Or God might be understood by the activist as the source of unrest in the world; that is, the vision of what we regard as divine, contrasted with the reality in which we live, mandates action to bring the ideal and the real closer together.

Required of any Unitarian Universalist social ethic is a grounding in a theological stance that prompts and sustains action on behalf of the Beloved Community. The materials for such a view are at least partially at hand. For James Luther Adams, a Christian theist, the God term could be replaced by the phrase "that which ultimately concerns humanity" or "that in which we should place our confidence." In *On Being Human Religiously,* he wrote,

God is . . . the inescapable, commanding reality that sustains and transforms all meaningful existence. . . . It is a working reality that every person is destined to live with. . . . This reality is, then, no human contrivance; it is a reality without which no human good can be realized and without which growth of meaning is impossible. Theists and religious humanists find common ground here. They differ in defining the context in which human existence and human good are to be understood.

Sharon Welch articulates a theology of immanence. "I argue that the divine is . . . relational power, and that it is neither necessary nor liberating to posit a substance or ground that exists outside of relational power. . . . The power of compassion is divine. . . . This power of compassion and anger is holy." Welch rejects ideas about God or the Goddess despite the comfort they may give. In her study of theodicy—how can evil exist in a world created by a loving God?—she finds that the triumph of evil undermines classic theism. "I find the god of classical theism irrational and unworthy of worship." Divinity for her is a "quality of relationships, lives, events, and natural processes that are worthy of worship, that provide orientation, focus, and guidance to our lives." This concept of the holy provides a transcendence that understands the complexity of life, can address the conditions of oppression that mark that life, and participates in a movement of social transformation. These social movements for justice are holy. "They are manifestations of transcendence, of the love of life and self leading to work for social change."

Henry Nelson Wieman incorporates these powers in his concept of creativity. What processes move us toward the good life in the Beloved Community? We cannot give ourselves in commitment to an indifferent universe nor to a cosmic consciousness, but rather to that creativity operating in the natural order and in human life that produces human value. This creativity is not a supernatural being, but a dynamic process that creates and sustains us, bringing into being a community of mutual support. Such a concept can be grasped by the human mind. Human meaning then is realizable within the context of human history.

In *Religious Inquiry: Some Explorations,* Wieman illustrates the point by analogy in his discussion of good health:

One of the most simple examples is good health. There is a reality operating to create good health. It is the biological organism. No man can create good health apart from the right functioning of his organism. The biological activities create the health. All our action can do is meet the demands of this organic creativity by eating food in right quantity and quality, breathing pure air, drinking pure water, taking exercise and the like. But all this "doing" of ours does not create the good health; it merely provides the conditions under which the biological processes can operate effectively in creating good health. There can be no life at all without the biological organism, and "health" merely means life operating without obstruction.

Wieman does not allow himself to be trapped by the theist–humanist debate. It is, he says, like the person who asks, when seeing an automobile for the first time, what makes it go? Does someone push it or is there a hidden horse pulling it? The answer is neither; rather, it is the exploding gasoline. "Creativity is not God in the traditional sense of that word. But neither does it operate under the control of human purpose." Creativity operates both in terms of the human mind and in terms of that which creates the human mind. "This is the kind of transcendence involved in religious commitment to the creativity operating in human existence."

So, for Wieman, ultimate reality has three dimensions: (1) It refers to the power of being out of which human life has emerged; (2) it sustains human existence; and (3) it is the ultimate meaning of human existence, human destiny. We have here what we might call "horizontal transcendence," a commitment to values greater than the self, emerging from a creativity among people but not relegated to the realm of the divine. Wieman suggests that the "mysterium tremendum" of such a theology is the full appreciation of the scope of creativity that exceeds our grasp. "Awareness of this unattainable reach of creativity is experience of the holy."

As a religious humanist I would affirm what the French writer Albert Camus calls the "benign indifference of the universe." In distinction to a biblical God who notes the fall of every sparrow, this humanist formulation of ultimate reality would point out that reality does not play favorites. "The rain falls on the just and on the unjust." We must live, as Camus phrases it, "without appeal." In this view, God's will becomes chiefly the human projection of human aspirations on a cosmic screen. Equating God's will with some merely human aspiration would seem the height of idolatry and a violation of the Protestant principle that asserts that nothing human is absolute. We must resist the temptation to look into the deep well of our psyches, see our mirror image in the water, and call it God. This reality can be seen to be benign, however, in the sense that there are creative powers in the cosmos, natural and human, that can be tapped to enhance the quality of human life.

Human History: The "For Instances" of Theology

Another important theological task for us to come to terms with is a sense of our history as biological and historical creatures, products of an evolutionary development, inheritors of a historical religious tradition and culminations of a personal life history. The values emerging from the transaction of self and history are a sense of identity with the human race in general and with a community of faith in particular, a sense of participation in the historical process itself.

Here is the interaction of the self with time over space and with the people, groups, and events that shape our world. The tasks of the religious self are to come to terms with history, both biological and cultural, to develop a sense of continuity with what has gone before, and, most important, to make a commitment to history as participant and change agent. We do this to rebut the caustic comment that all the world's a stage and all the men and women merely drama critics.

Unitarian Universalists have inherited from the Jewish and Christian traditions a philosophy of history that is linear in nature, moving from "proton" to "eschaton," from beginning to end. This is in distinction to an Eastern cyclical history or to an eclipse of history by a focus on self and cosmos alone. This is the prophetic understanding of history. As noted before, liberals have been lopsidedly optimistic in their historical orientation and have spoken of the perfectibility of human nature and society. This does not mean simply that evil can emerge from history, but that often evil and good emerge side by side from the same roots. In *On Being Human Religiously*, James Luther Adams wrote,

> When we say that history is tragic, we mean that the perversions and failures of history are associated precisely with the highest creative powers of humanity and thus with our greatest achievements. . . . The national culture, for example, is the soil from which issue cherished treasures of a people, their language, their poetry, their music, their common social heritage. Yet nationalism is also one of the most destructive forces in the whole of human history.

Unitarian Universalists, however, have continually stressed the potential for good. But the good is neither automatic nor inevitable.

Furthermore, we need to ask if history has an ultimate meaning. For the Christian it does, couched in terms of the Kingdom of God. My humanist position is well stated by Camus: "I continue to believe that this world has no ultimate meaning. But I know that something in it has a meaning and that is man, because he is the only creature to insist on having one. This world has at least the truth of man, and our task is to provide its justification against fate itself."

I do not find any ultimate meaning in history, no overall direction or pattern apart from what humanity imposes on it. So, for the religious humanist the human task is not to discover ultimate meaning written into history, but to create human meaning out of it. Hence the humanist can envision no eschaton, but rather envisions history as an ongoing drama in which historical meaning is not discovered through divine revelation, but created through human effort. Thus the goal of ethical effort in history is couched in human, not divine, terms. The historical task of the religious humanist is not the ushering in of the Kingdom of God and certainly not preparing for the eschatological entrance of God into human history; it is serving the values that expand the quality of life on the planet. Historical meaning can be seen as an open-ended process of meliorism or, as it is so graphically stated in Jewish tradition, *Tikkun ha' olam*, to repair the world. Human history, then, is the fundamental arena for action and meaning. Moving toward the Beloved Community is the meaning of history.

The Kingdom of God, while a powerful image, is not a particularly appropriate end-in-view for the religious humanist. It refers to a tradition in which many Unitarian Universalists do not feel comfortable; it is royalist, having been developed in predemocratic times; it is chauvinistic in its male imagery, which makes it an exclusionary rather than an inclusive construct. For the religious humanist the Beloved Community of Love and Justice or the Beloved Community of Earth would be a more appropriate end-in-view. Community implies some sense of voluntary cooperation in working out social arrangements (democracy); justice is the ordering principle in social arrangements; love is the ultimate goal of interpersonal relationships in such a community.

Participation in the process is crucial here, for the religious humanist sees history as an ongoing process that is radically open-ended. It may end tomorrow by human or natural action, or it may continue indefinitely beyond our wildest imagination. There is no confidence in a suprahuman historical force. Here is the humanist's tragic view of history.

William Jones states it this way in *Is God a White Racist?*:

> The humanist argues that we must act as if history were open-ended and multivalued, as if our human choices and actions were determinative for human destiny. . . . There does not appear to be an inevitable historical development, sponsored by ultimate reality, that can be confidently demonstrated. Rather, value possibilities are equally probable; oppression and liberation are equal options. Nor is there a cosmic life-guard to save humanity from its self-destructive choices.

That this view is generally accepted by Unitarian Universalists is illustrated in the 1967 denominational Committee on Goals survey, in which 58.8% of the respondents denied that there is a "power which works in history through man that transforms evil into good." History is fully and radically in human hands. We might borrow a leaf from Karl Marx's notebook and say that the philosophers have only interpreted the world; the point is to change it.

Therefore, I affirm what I call horizontal transcendence. I look to no God in or beyond history as a point of reference. My point of reference is the Beloved Community, a concept that transcends my meager efforts, a vision sufficiently sublime that I do not confuse it with reality, a goal that commands my allegiance. Those who work for social justice are too often preoccupied with finite endeavors, which are dirty with the everyday, dingy with the prosaic, somehow separated from the cosmic connection. The task is to learn to live with the partial fulfillment of a just and sustainable world, recognizing that we are finite creatures who aspire infinitely. Our task is unfinished just as the cosmic creativity is ever in process.

As Sharon Welch says, "The horizon of action is recognition that we cannot imagine how we will win. . . . we cannot guarantee decisive changes in the near future or even in our lifetime. . . . The eschatological reservation is the reminder that all of our good works are partial." She nevertheless envisions a Beloved Community "of justice and joy."

The social activist needs to place the quest for justice in a larger framework than the immediate. Our efforts to change the world are projected against a cosmic screen of ultimate concern. There is a creating, sustaining, transforming, commanding creativity at work in the cosmos of which we are part. This creativity transcends us in the sense that we had no part in the creation of the natural world. The cosmic order swirls about us quite independently. Through the workings of the natural order, the thrust of evolution, it transforms the world. And so the religious question becomes, What can we contribute to the Beloved Community?

And so, in the beginning was the Word and the Word was with God, and the word was God. And we are authors of the word. We are authors, coauthors with the Nameless One, of the world. There is a cosmic connection, and we are part of the warp and weft of it. We may be cosmically alone, but we are humanly together.

Ethics as Meeting Unenforceable Obligations

A further critical task is defining the relationship of the self to others, referring to individual and corporate others and that nonpersonal other, the natural environment. The value norm operating in interpersonal relations is love; in intergroup relations, justice; in relating to the natural environment, trusteeship; all held together by the fundamental ethic of reverence for life. Psychologically speaking, this is ego-extension, the process of expanding interests beyond the self and identifying with them.

In the day-to-day of our living, we are obliged to consider our relationships, not with history as an abstraction, but with the flesh and blood people with whom we live and work. Ethics are "unenforceable obligations," according to Rushworth Kidder. If "laws are the wise restraints that make us free," says James Conant, then ethics are the inner imperatives that prompt us to care when we need not, to act when it may be controversial, to serve when we would rather indulge ourselves. The true test of character is to act when so doing will not do us any personal good.

Hosea Ballou, a nineteenth-century Universalist preacher of universal salvation, was riding the circuit in the New Hampshire hills with a Baptist minister one afternoon. They argued theology as they traveled. At one point, the Baptist looked over and said, "Brother Ballou, if I were a Universalist and feared not the fires of hell, I could hit you over the head, steal your horse and saddle, and ride away, and I'd still go to heaven." Hosea Ballou looked over at him and said, "If you were a Universalist, the idea would never occur to you."

The most characteristic ethics of American culture at the cusp of the twentieth and twenty-first centuries cause baby-boomers to be labeled the IDI generation, the "I deserve it generation." There is a dangerous self-centeredness abroad that, for example, enables the rich to get richer while the poor get poorer. The so-called "fortunate fifth," the wealthiest twenty percent of the population, has seemingly lost any concern it might have had for the poorest twenty percent. The gap between the most affluent and the middle class is also growing.

Robert Coles in *The Moral Life of Children* writes, "Something is wrong with a society whose members are endlessly preoccupied with feeling better, rather than obsessed with making the world better." In his cross-cultural studies of children, he finds that the self-portraits of rich American children fill up the whole page, while in those of Hopi Indian children of the American Southwest they are merely a dot in a rich landscape.

To help in an understanding of Unitarian Universalist ethics, I suggest the metaphor of a moral compass that indicates factors guiding moral decision making. A compass does not tell us exactly what to do, but does help us find our bearings.

The first point: Our final authority for moral decision making is neither church nor state, but ourselves as moral actors. This approach is not solipsism in which an unconnected ego arbitrarily makes moral judgments, unable to see the forest for the ME's, as it has been put. In the on-the-ground existential reality in which we live, we must make our moral decisions, even if we simply defer to some external authority. The Roman Catholic chooses to accept or not accept the authority of the pope. Ultimately, we must affirm our own authority and accept our responsibility.

The seventeenth-century French philosopher La Rochefoucauld trenchantly suggests a second point on the moral compass, motivation. "However brilliant an action, it should not be esteemed great unless the result of a great motive." This is what I call "the importance of being good for nothing." My motive to be good ought not be based on anticipated reward, nor ought my temptation to do evil be stifled by feared punishment. We ought to do good for the sake of doing good; this is motive enough.

A third point: The moral agent must take responsibility for the results of action. In the delightful though deeply troubling film by the late Peter Sellers, *Heavens Above,* the star is vicar of a small church in a contented English village flourishing under the benevolence of the wealthy Despard family and the pill it manufactures, a "sedative, pepper-upper and laxative combined, a perfect trinity." When Sellers applies the New Testament ethic of selling what we have and giving to the poor, riotous anarchy occurs, driving butcher, baker, and candlestick maker out of business. The sincere vicar did not take account of the consequences of his behavior. We must do so, no matter how well-intentioned we are.

What is going on here? The moral situation is a fourth point of moral decision making. This factor questions the belief that moral rules are good in all times and all places for all people. Most of us would agree that it is wrong to kill another human being. Yet extremists of the antiabortion movement morally justify murdering doctors and escorts at abortion clinics. They are wrong because the undisputed actual harm far outweighs whatever potential harm they think they prevent on a disputed issue.

Ends and means is a traditional ethical dilemma. There is the case of Pastor Dietrich Bonhoffer, who took part in a plot to assassinate Hitler. He maintained that murder is never right, but sometimes we must set aside principle and do the right thing—stop genocide. Ethicists call this the "teleological suspension of the ethical"; some ends *(telos)* are so transcendent that we must violate the ordinary rules. There is danger here on the slippery slope and we have to be extremely careful. "Does the end ever justify the means?" is a logical extension of this issue.

Most of us make moral decisions based on values. But what if these values come into conflict? For instance, I once led an adult education program in which we discussed moral dilemmas that participants faced in the workaday world. One told of a researcher friend who had made what he thought was a breakthrough in medical science. However, his company would neither proceed, because it was not in their product line, nor let him take it elsewhere, because they claimed it was their intellectual property. Should the researcher violate his contract to help humanity?

And, finally, the issue of character, that sense of integrity in which the inner and outer person are the same, the consistency of good living over a lifetime, the sense that one seeks to live the good life for its own sake. Society depends on such basic human decency because there are not enough morality or law enforcers to guide and govern behavior unless most of the people most of the time honor moral obligations without thought of reward or punishment.

Evangelist Dwight Moody had it right, I believe, when he said, "Character is what you are in the dark." We are what we do and we do what we are. Character is the Abraham Lincoln who legend says walked miles to return three cents he had inadvertently overcharged a customer. It is the prisoner of war refusing to betray comrades even though no one will know. It is the Jean Valjean of *Les Miserables* fame who exudes decency despite a fate that conspired against him.

Liberal religious morality happens when we recognize with T. S. Eliot "the perpetual struggle of Good and Evil." When we eschew the simple dogmas of Religious Right ethics, we are engaging in a form of moral orienteering by internal compass.

We Are the Meaning Makers

Finally, one of our central tasks is to clarify what meaning or meanings life has for us. What are the purposes for which we live? The values emerging out of a dialogue of the self with its deeper self would be a sense of justification, transcending purposes for which one labors, or, to use a more traditional theological term, salvation, in the sense of becoming whole.

In his discussion of logotherapy, Viktor Frankl posits three sources of human meaning: (1) the intrinsic worth of human experiences of love and beauty; (2) the capacity to endure suffering; and (3) participation in serving a cause that is greater than the self. It is the third source of meaning that is of central concern for a social ethic.

I submit that a vital source of personal religious meaning emerges out of commitment to causes that transcend the self. Psychologist Abraham Maslow has developed the concept of self-actualization, a very popular, but often misunderstood construction. He speaks of *deficiency needs*, requirements for security, status, and love, without which we could not survive. These blend into *being needs* as we mature, the need to grow, to transcend the self, to serve causes beyond the self, to discover life meaning. Maslow wrote, "Self-actualizing people are, without one single exception, involved in a cause outside their own skin, in some thing outside themselves. They are devoted, working at something, something which is very precious to them—some calling or vocation in the old sense, the priestly sense."

As we embrace the spiritual, we need to remember that a vital source of religious meaning is through our participation in the actions and passions of our time. A convictional theology provides personal meaning. Without the empowerment of a theological vision, our actions often lack total commitment; our staying power is limited; we become victims of the demonic of privatization; we experience moral and spiritual burnout. I affirm what James Luther Adams calls the "pragmatic theory of meaning." Meaning emerges in lived human experience.

William Butler Yeats wrote, "Things fall apart, the center cannot hold. The best lack all conviction and the worst are full of passionate intensity." To regain the center and to rekindle passionate intensity are what convictional theology seeks. It becomes what James Luther Adams calls our "centerstance in the midst of circumstance," a place to stand in the midst of a world that seems to have lost its way.

To work for the Beloved Community is simply part of what it means to be a Unitarian Universalist. Faith exists by mission as a fire exists by burning. I conclude that the theological rootage for a Unitarian Universalist social gospel is present in this pragmatic theory of meaning. In response to the Christian debate over whether salvation is by works or by faith, the Unitarian Universalist response has been "salvation by character." That is, a sense of self-justification, a sense of purpose and meaning emerge not out of earning merit by good works, nor out of God's freely given grace, but out of what the person becomes behaviorally as an acting whole. All of us need a sense of significance that we have been here, that we mattered, that we made a difference by living.

The French writer Antoine de Saint-Exupery states it poetically: "To be [human] is, precisely, to be responsible. It is to feel shame at the sight of what seems to be unmerited misery. It is to take pride in a victory won by one's comrades. It is to feel, when setting one's stone, that one is contributing to the building of the world."

CHAPTER FIVE

A Covenant of
Unenforceable Obligations

Charles Taylor, former secretary of the American Association of Theological Schools, told a troubling story about a conversation with a theological ethicist in a major German university shortly after World War II. In the course of the conversation the professor patted a massive manuscript on his desk and announced that he had just completed a work on ethics and society, and it was a truly theological work—entirely unaffected by anything that had happened during the last century or two.

If theology is history teaching by example, then this narrative must be a warning. It is imperative we seek theological depth without sacrificing social relevance, endeavoring to keep the theoretical and the pragmatic in creative tension. This attempt rests on the observation of Aristotle that "one becomes a courageous person, is trained in moral virtue, only by engaging in courageous deeds."

Ideas have consequences; clarity of thought is a *sine qua non* of accuracy in action. My hope is that Unitarian Universalist congregations enter the new millennium inspired by a new social gospel, calling on the virtues of that turn-of-the-century movement but learning from its mistakes. The old social gospel had an exaggerated optimism with regard to human nature and a somewhat naive sentimentalism for social change. In sum, it could not survive reality.

A direct response to those weaknesses was Reinhold Niebuhr's critique of liberalism and a resulting balance-of-power ethic. Niebuhr articulated a more sober assessment of human nature and a more realistic view of the possibilities of human history. He sought a social situation in which a balance of powers might bring an approximation of justice. While appreciating and utilizing the Niebuhrian analysis, I believe we can move beyond his *realpolitik* to a social ethic informed by a chastened religious humanism and the insights of liberation theology and then integrate them into a liberal religious theological context. A social ethic for our day must be fundamentally a theological social ethic. It must reflect on matters of ultimate importance. This ethic must furnish insights for humane living in the social, political, and economic currents of our time, but always in the light of some ultimate commitment that we have chosen to make our own. If we understand this, liberal religion has the ethical resources to sustain the prophetic imperative.

"To be is to be for others." These words of Unitarian Universalist theologian Gene Reeves describe the essence of ethics. Morality begins when preoccupation with the self gives way to interest in the welfare of others. Yet it is exceedingly hard to be a moral creature, and we are in need of both inspiration and guidance. This is especially true of a religious movement that does not live under the divine imperative of inerrant scripture, omniscient church, and infallible leaders. However, to be cast adrift on a sea of philosophical nihilism, theological emptiness, and ethical anarchy is no alternative. We need to discover and develop a social ethic that can express our prophetic imperative. Liberal religion in its Unitarian Universalist form is a covenantal, prophetic community of free and disciplined men and women working toward the Beloved Community of Love and Justice.

ETHICS AS UNENFORCEABLE OBLIGATIONS

A liberal religious social ethic must be evolving, not absolute. James Luther Adams wrote in *On Being Human Religiously*,

> Now it should be clear that if some people wish infallible guidance in religion, they are not going to find it in liberal religion. . . . They [orthodox mentors] sometimes tell us that the mortal sin of the liberal is the unwillingness to submit to divine authority and that this unwillingness grows out of intellectual pride. What the orthodox overlooks, however, is this: the most pretentious pride of all is that of the man who thinks himself capable of recognizing infallibility, for he must himself claim to be infallible in order to identify the infallible.

Humanist Walter Kaufmann adds, "The main objection to absolute morality is that even if there were absolute moral standards we should have no way of knowing whether we had found them."

"Everything nailed down is coming loose," said the Angel Gabriel, looking down on humanity's moral confusion in Marc Connelly's 1930 play *The Green Pastures.* This classic American drama translates biblical drama into very earthy terms. Gabriel's sad words are as accurate now as they were in 1930.

We live in an age of moral deconstructionism—we fearlessly critique and criticize, dissect and dismantle our culture's conventional wisdom in which the Ten Commandments are paramount. The Decalogue was a kind of constitutional law for a wandering people. Biblical scholars believe there were ten to correspond to the ten fingers, thus making them easier to memorize for public worship. They stand as a major ethical step forward in their time, some three thousand years ago.

To what extent are they still instructive? Most of us would reject a jealous god who equates blasphemy with murder. This Jehovah by and large was not a user-friendly god, but a vain and vengeful one who promised retribution for every violation of the commandments. This god is the great ethical enforcer. Humanity was simply to obey or be punished. For many of us this great enforcer concept has lost its power; we no longer believe in God as a supreme lawgiver.

I recall one summer evening many years ago when a Roman Catholic visitor, learning I was a minister, asked about my religion. When he learned that I neither feared hell nor sought heaven, but believed in "the importance of being good—for nothing," he was incredulous. He said that if he didn't fear eternal punishment or seek eternal reward there would be no telling what he would do. He was bound to the great enforcer, not the moral power of unenforceable obligations.

Why do we continue to work for justice even when we are at times so discouraged? Why do we give money to causes when we know that the groups we support will be greatly outspent by the powers and principalities of the world? Why do we continue to work for justice when it so often opens us up to criticism? Why do we seek peace when no one pressures or rewards us, and it would be much more satisfying to go and cultivate our gardens or otherwise indulge ourselves? Why do we involve ourselves in community service and social action when no one seems to care and we often fail? And why have people done these things for centuries? No external power is forcing us to meet these obligations; we are truly on our own, moved not by the "cudgel but an inward music: the irresistible power of unarmed truth, the powerful attraction of its example," in Boris Pasternak's words. Character is what we are when no one is looking. Character is when we act though it will not do us any particular good. Character is when we respond to our unenforceable obligations to our neighbors, near or far.

Nonetheless, no responsible religious social ethic can retreat to a situationist approach without universal principles. It is my contention that reverence for life is the ordering principle for a liberal religious social ethic, that reverence for life gives rise to a moral imperative for love in interpersonal relationships, justice in social relationships, and trusteeship in our relationships with our environment.

REVERENCE FOR LIFE

Reverence for life was the central principle of Albert Schweitzer's philosophy of civilization, which is described in *The Ethical Mysticism of Albert Schweitzer* by Henry Clark. It is useful for a religious humanist social ethic because it is naturalistic, derived from our very nature as human beings. Schweitzer believed that reverence for life emerges out of our fundamental will to live. "The essential thing to realize about ethics is that it is the very manifestation of our will-to-live. . . . Whence this universe came, or whither it is bound, or how it happens to be at all, knowledge cannot tell me. Only this: that the will-to-live is everywhere present, even as in me."

We then ask the question about our attitudes toward this other life. Since others appear to be much like us, we intuitively know other life possesses this same will to live. That which is evil is that which annihilates, hampers, or hinders life; that which is good is the saving or serving of life, enabling it to attain its highest development.

This ethic is rational because it results in reflection upon life. It is dependent on no special revelation or even any particular religious tradition, but on the rational minds of human beings. It is universal in that it relates to every form of life, as Schweitzer puts it, "seeking so far as possible to refrain from destroying any life, regardless of its particular type." It is absolute in the sense that "we are responsible for the lives of those about us," although it "does not lay down specific rules for each possible situation." It is a discriminating ethic, for it recognizes human life as the most important life we know. Choices must be made as to what life shall be saved and what life destroyed. Reverence for life involves active trusteeship for enhancing life.

Reverence for life becomes the central motif in what has been called *eco-justice* (justice held together with ecology). Such an ecological ethic recognizes human beings as simply one link in "the great living system," as John Ruskin Clark calls it in his book of the same title. This is our "respect for the interdependent web of all existence of which we are a part." Not incidentally, Rachel Carson, whose *Silent*

Spring arguably launched the environmental movement, dedicated her book to Albert Schweitzer.

Our reverence for all life comes from a realization that we are part of life. There is a sense of solidarity in the realization that we are made of the same stuff as stars, photons, and the beasts of the field. Schweitzer continues, "In the very fibers of our being, we bear within ourselves the fact of the solidarity of life." Out of this recognition of material identity with all that is comes a spiritual sense of a mystic oneness with being, "for this material-born ethic becomes engraved upon our hearts, and culminates in spiritual union and harmony with the Creative Will which is in and through all."

Love as *agape*, self-giving love, is a judgment on every social form. Love as care, knowledge, respect, and responsibility is the central value in interpersonal relations. However, this concept will not be developed here. While love is the noblest virtue in personal relations between individuals, justice is the primary value in social relations among groups. Each of us is a sinner in the sense of missing the mark, being creatures of finite freedom; nevertheless our individual moral potential is still greater than that of the group. The group is a collective egoism, composed of many individual egoisms reinforcing one another. The group has even less potential for moral behavior than has the individual, since it is usually powerful enough to defy social restraints. There are also fewer inner moral restraints operating in the group, and there tends to be less reason to check and guide impulse. Within the group it is more difficult to achieve consensus, and there is far less capacity to comprehend the needs of others. The group, unlike the individual, cannot transcend itself. Unlike the individual, without the power of reason, the group finds it much more difficult to engage in the rational self-criticism so necessary for moral growth. Thus, while ethical relations are possible between persons, the relations between groups are more aptly described as political.

There is a classic illustration of this in John Steinbeck's novel *The Grapes of Wrath*. An Oklahoma farmer is about to see his farm bulldozed to the ground as the bank forecloses on his mortgage. He asks the driver who is responsible. When he hears "the bank," he asks, "Who is the bank?" There is no answer, for the bank in an impersonal collective, composed of individuals who do not even know the individual story of the poor farmer. The bank directors function, not as moral agents, but as functionaries in a collective manner. They make seemingly abstract political and economic decisions apparently unaware of their personal implications.

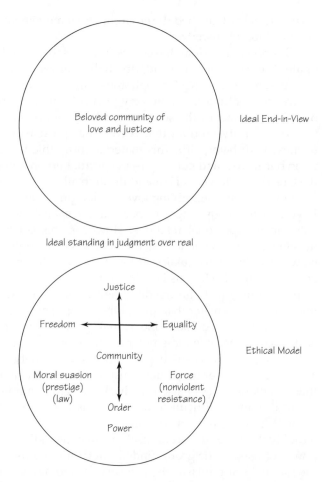

Beloved community of
love and justice

Ideal End-in-View

Ideal standing in judgment over real

Justice

Freedom ← → Equality

Community

Moral suasion
(prestige)
(law)

Force
(nonviolent
resistance)

Order

Power

Ethical Model

The Beloved Community: A Social Ethical Model

The above figure is a schema of the Beloved Community. The Beloved Community is a transcendent symbol that has evocative power to rally our spirits and energies to the cause of justice. It includes humanists and theists, as well as others of different theological persuasions. It is, I contend, the highest common denominator for Unitarian Universalists and thus an appropriate symbol for us. The Beloved Community is an ideal end-in-view transcending historical reality. It is an image embodying human hopes and standing over against human finitude in judgment of the social order.

This community's basic characteristic is human solidarity, a concept given expression by Martin Luther King, Jr., as described by Kenneth L. Smith and Ira G. Zepp, Jr., in *Search for the Beloved Community: The Thinking of Martin Luther King, Jr.* It is curious that King, coming from the Christian black church tradition, did not use the more traditional Kingdom of God instead of the image of the Beloved Community in his writing. He was perhaps more liberal theologically than we had thought.

The church is the microcosm of the Beloved Community, seeking to embody the principles of love and justice in its own life. This, however, is inadequate to fulfill the role of the prophetic church. Ideally, the religion of this Beloved Community in miniature overflows in action upon the public realm. The Beloved Community is the historical and ethical ideal end-in-view upon which the liberal church as corporate agent is built.

Justice

Justice is posited as the criterion for human good in the social order, justice recognizing the inherent worth of human personality and seeking to secure the well-being of each; i.e., expanding the quality of life. In ethical terms we are mandated to treat persons as ends, not means.

Former Unitarian Universalist Association president William F. Schulz tells this story, which is indicative of the inherent worth and dignity of every person.

> Father Jeremiah was an old monk who lived for more than five decades in the Coptic Monastery of St. Macarius. One day a visitor chanced upon that remote monastery, a visitor of Anglican persuasion—no Coptic he. Jeremiah greeted the visitor with all the warmth and hospitality one would presume to be reserved for a saint. The visitor, having expected to be treated for the heretic he was, was astounded by Jeremiah's generosity and asked the reason. The old monk threw back his head and laughed. "My friend," he said, "in this monastery we always treat guests as angels—just in case!"

Justice is judged by freedom, equity, and community.

Freedom

Freedom is the capacity of individuals and groups to pursue their interests and goals: self-determination. As such, freedom is a social value more than a personal one. It is significant only in a human community. Freedom is never absolute, but always carries with it a strong sense of social responsibility. Freedom is limited, as when it interferes with the freedom of others (the "clear and present danger" doctrine in which yelling "fire" in a crowded theater is not socially permissible freedom).

Freedom as self-determination is critical as a principle of justice. It is the maximum opportunity for the individual to actualize creative freedom: liberty. This is in no sense the mere absence of external compulsion. Both political tyranny and poverty restrict self-determination, the former by direct, coercive means and the latter by diminishing the range of choices for self-actualization. Freedom, then, is not merely the lack of external restriction. It also involves the availability of choices. Hence, the quality of freedom is enhanced as choices are expanded and deepened and made accessible to decision makers.

For example, at the 1981 Cancun Conference on the North–South Dialogue, twenty-two world leaders gathered to discuss world poverty in a luxury resort not far from a Mexican slum. Resisting efforts to conduct this dialogue in a United Nations setting, President Ronald Reagan extolled the free market as the solution to global poverty. He cited the Chinese saying, "Give a man a fish and you feed him for a day; teach a man to fish and he feeds himself for a lifetime." Nigeria's representative Shagari attached a postscript. "I agree there is an object lesson here. I must hasten to add, however, that the man has to be supplied with hooks and nets in order to put into practice his invaluable knowledge of fishing."

Freedom is not an end in itself, but rather, as Martin Buber said, "Freedom is a footbridge, not a dwelling place. It cannot be dispensed with and it cannot be made use of in itself; without it nothing succeeds, but neither does anything succeed by means of it; it is the run before the jump, the tuning of the violin, . . . the confirmation of that primal and mighty potentiality which it cannot even begin to actualize."

Freedom creates the place of possibility for making choices that enhance the quality of life. James Luther Adams points out that freedom means that relations between persons must be based on "mutual, free consent, not coercion, though that freedom can never be absolute. Persuasion can be perverted into a camouflage for duress. Nevertheless, free choice is a principle without which religion, or society, or politics, cannot be liberal."

Equity

Equity conveys the sense of fairness, equal access to the necessary material and spiritual goods of life so as to provide security for all. It is an arrangement of social patterns dividing the privileges of the common human enterprise fairly to each. Equity is summed up in an incisive aphorism, attributed to Mahatma Gandhi: "There is enough to meet everyone's need, but not everyone's greed." We need only look at our own nation to see the increasing gap between rich and poor, even between rich and middle class, in both income and wealth. Inequality on a global scale is even more dramatic—and tragic. The problem is not production, but distribution; the issue is not technical, but moral. We are caught in the iron rule of maldistribution.

In *A Feminist Ethic of Risk*, Sharon Welch writes of the

despair of the affluent, the despair of the middle class . . . cushioned by privilege and grounded in privilege. It is easier to give up on long-term social change when one is comfortable in the present—when it is possible to have challenging work, excellent health care and housing, and access to the fine arts. . . . It masks the bad faith of abandoning social justice work for others when one is already the beneficiary of partial social change. . . . Few middle-class activists are aware of the economic and political factors constitutive of our experience.

I contend that this inequity is inherently unjust, not only because poverty denies basic human needs and rights to the poor, but also because wealth addiction tends to corrupt the moral and spiritual life of the rich. Wealth insulates us from the pain of poverty; it enables us to deny the humanness of the poor. This injustice struck me some years ago as I returned from a meeting of the Unitarian Universalist Service Committee board of directors. I read a UNICEF report about 42,000 children dying needlessly each day alongside a *Wall Street Journal* article about American business executives, whose incomes were in six figures (this was in the early eighties) and who were worried about their financial futures.

Minimally, society must provide basic security in subsistence needs. Such security involves the opportunity to actualize creative freedom. It requires means for the cultivation of the spirit. Both poverty and wealth are corrupting. Poverty corrupts because it breeds anxiety, fear, helplessness, worthlessness, powerlessness. But wealth also corrupts, because it breeds insensitivity, and it produces poverty through exploitation.

Equity here does not refer to genetic equality. It refers to true equality of opportunity to have access to the material and spiritual goods of the society. This must involve some semblance of equal education, employment, and treatment. To quote the United Nations Universal Declaration of Human Rights, Article 2:

> Everyone has the right to a standard of living adequate for the health and well-being of himself and of his family, including food, clothing, housing, and medical care and necessary social services, and the right to security in the event of unemployment, sickness, disability, widowhood, old age or other lack of livelihood in circumstances beyond his control.

Greed and gluttony are currently alive and well alongside poverty and powerlessness. Instead of a theology of sufficiency for all, we have settled on poverty for the masses, superfluity for the elite. As Confucius is reputed to have said, "To centralize wealth is to disperse the people; to distribute wealth is to collect the people."

A classic cartoon sets the problem. Three fish are swimming one behind the other. The smallest, in the lead, says "There is no justice." Behind, its mouth open to devour the first fish, is a second larger fish which says, "There is some justice." Behind it swims a still larger fish with mouth open to devour both, saying, "The world is just." But the world is not just. This is the problem to which a new social gospel must address itself.

Community

Community is a third principle of justice. Being part of a community means being part of a group in which persons treat others as ends, not means to some political, economic, or social goal. In this community is the possibility for I–thou relationships as contrasted with I–it relationships.

The key to community is relationship, a concept brought to the fore with great force by feminist theologians. I agree with Sharon Welch that "the divine is that relational power, and that it is neither necessary nor liberating to posit a substance or ground that exists outside of relational power." The divine for her—and for me—is the quality of these relationships, whether or not there is a sense of solidarity in the community.

As T. S. Eliot puts it in *Choruses from the Rock*, "When the stranger says, 'What is the meaning of this city? Do you huddle close together because you love each other?' What will you answer? 'No, we all dwell together to make money from each other' or 'This is a community'?" Liberal religion must resist its flirtation with a radical autonomy if we are to construct a social ethic that is transformative, that both recognizes and creates human solidarity. In community there is responsibility which each has for all and all have for each.

Albert Schweitzer illustrates this solidarity with a homely anecdote: A flock of wild geese had settled to rest on a pond. One of the flock was captured by a gardener, who clipped its wings before releasing it. When the geese started to resume their flight, this one tried frantically, but vainly, to lift itself into the air. The others, observing his struggles, flew about in obvious efforts to encourage him; but it was no use. Thereupon, the entire flock settled back on the pond and waited until the damaged feathers had grown sufficiently to permit the goose to fly. Meanwhile, the unethical gardener, having been converted by the ethical geese, gladly watched them as they finally rose together and all resumed their long flight.

The principles of freedom, equity, and community interact with one another. Capitalism may be seen as an example of a form of social organization that stresses freedom over equity and community, while socialism represents a form valuing equity and community over freedom. The former stresses individualism; the latter, community. The ideal is a balance in which they can inform one another and so serve as joint standards for justice. Equal justice represents a tension between what the individual or group desires (self-determination) and the interests and desires of the other (the common good).

Justice, however, cannot be achieved in the midst of chaos; there must be social order. Order gained through peace and justice yields community. Order through force yields inherent instability. Order cannot be maintained as long as there is injustice in the society. Without peace there is no justice; without justice there is no peace. True community solidarity comes only when there is peace with justice.

Take the dilemma faced by Abraham Lincoln during the Civil War. Lincoln was willing to have the Union exist half-slave and half-free, but it soon became apparent that this was impossible. Order and community could not be maintained under the injustice of slavery. There are basically two ways to preserve order and to achieve the authority required to govern effectively, the prestige of justice and the use of force. Sometimes the former is enough to preserve harmony; Lincoln necessarily chose the latter. This symbolizes the truth that order must undergird justice in the community, but only an order that implies justice will survive.

Harvard philosopher John Rawls has written of justice as fairness, positing a simulation game in which the players are engaged in the creation of a new society but live behind a veil of ignorance. None knows how they will fare in the new dispensation. Knowing that, they are admonished to create a fair society. How much freedom, how much equality, how much justice would they grant if they did not know their own outcome in the coming scheme of things? What would be fair? To give content to that fairness is the task of justice-makers in the Beloved Community.

Power

A critical category for ethical reflection is power. Hugo Hollerorth, in his philosophical statement on Unitarian Universalist religious education, wrote, "To be a human being is to be a dwelling place of power. To move about the world and interact with it is to encounter power. . . . Religion arises, then, out of the effort of human beings to make their way in a world of conflicting powers."

The individual is a center of power—not only individual power to direct the course of our individual lives, but of social power, the capacity to participate in making social decisions that affect us. Power, unfortunately, is fraught with negative connotations: the will to power, domination, exploitation, manipulation, who gets what when, where, and how? We think of Machiavelli's discussion of political power in *The Prince*. But power is actually an expression of the life of the self. It is the means by which the self asserts its very being. Socially, power is the means by which persons participate in the process of social decision making that affects their lives. Religion's question to power is "Why?"

While Lord Acton's axiom about power tending to corrupt and absolute power corrupting absolutely is a moral assumption, it is likewise true that impotence also tends to corrupt and absolute impotence corrupts absolutely. When a person or group lacks power to influence the society of which they are a part, there ensues corruption of the spirit, loss of a sense of self, and deprivation of a feeling of historical participation. James Luther Adams cites a small, all-white Appalachian community, Granny's Hollow, in eastern Kentucky. Having become the castoffs of a technological society, being powerless to change their condition, "disease, filth, malnutrition, illiteracy, inbreeding and its consequences, drunkenness, and religious fanaticism are rife among them." The Granny's Hollow story suggests the social necessity for a group to have social power to assert its own basic interests.

The foregoing analysis suggests that power must respect the inherent worth of individuals, and their self-determination must be expressed nonviolently. Change agents should emulate the aggressive utilization of nonviolent power in the style of Gandhi and King, rather than that of Henry David Thoreau, who employed passive resistance but did not use it as an effective tool for social change. Moral suasion through education and exercise of power through law must be exhausted before even contemplating a resort to force.

The concept of power *with* as contrasted with power *over* is another insight of feminist theology. In attacking hierarchies of power, feminists have found their own power in solidarity. It is a solidarity that marks liberation theology in all its forms—African American, Third World, Latin American, Asian. It is the richness of power as expressed by Riane Eisler in *The Chalice and the Blade,* a thoughtful metaphor for contrasting the basic presuppositions of power with and power over. The chalice symbolizes the common cup of communion, while the blade insinuates the divisive insertion of violence into relationships. While recognizing that the power over motif continues to dominate global society, it is power with and its democratic overtones that should be the goal of a liberal religious social ethic. Practically speaking, activists will need to live in the creative tension between the reality of social power and the idea of the partnership way.

A Unitarian Universalist Covenant for Social Responsibility

The concept of covenant historically has meant a formula, originating as the legal basis of society and used to describe the special relationship between God and people. In early Israelite society it was a legal agreement between people and between groups that made peaceful relationships possible. As the biblical drama unfolded, it became a special relationship of the Hebrew people with Yahweh. "And the Lord said to Moses, 'Write these words; in accordance with these words I have made a covenant with you and with Israel'" (Exodus 34:27). The people were chosen by God, not for special privileges but for special responsibility as a servant people; i.e., there are both promise and responsibility.

In the Hebrew scriptures, righteousness is primarily exhibited in the maintenance of the covenant, while sin is its transgression, a breach of the agreement. Different interpretations of the meaning of covenant are in evidence: the priestly emphasis on keeping the law and the prophetic emphasis on a covenant "written in the heart" (Jeremiah), which issue in righteous action. In the Christian scriptures the primary stress is a comparison of the Hebrew covenant of law and the New Testament covenant with Jesus as the Christ. In the history of the Christian church the covenanted community becomes a voluntary association of people who have a special loyalty and responsibility to

God. It consists of God's grace and the human promise to live in that grace consonant with the divine will.

What meaning can the concept of covenant have for Unitarian Universalists today? The central motif of covenant is the idea of a binding commitment. A covenant is not a contract—a legal agreement between parties in which each gets what each wants, a mutually beneficial agreement that can be voided if violated. A covenant is an ultimate commitment, a binding, life-orienting promise to be and to do certain things out of gratitude for what we receive—the gift of life.

The need for a social responsibility covenant in the liberal churches is especially strong since the liberal religious absence of binding theological, ethical, or social creeds can threaten us with organizational anarchy. A false understanding of freedom as liberty to believe or do anything we please without consideration of the community threatens the liberal church with social impotence. The lack of a spiritually focusing, ethically gripping value system may well render us incapable of concerted action. Those who fall for anything stand for nothing.

To take one historical example. Unitarian and other liberal religious groups did not have a good record of opposing Hitler in Nazi Germany. The prophets of opposition came from the Confessing Church, pastors like Martin Niemoeller and Dietrich Bonhoffer. An exception to this critique is the Unitarian Service Committee's work with refugees from 1938 on. Nonetheless, the historical record shows much left to have been desired. James Luther Adams quotes Karl Jaspers in a 1936 critique of religious liberalism in general: "Religious liberalism today has no positive significance because as a corporate movement it has no stamina and no discipline. I would counsel any young religious liberal training for the Protestant ministry to adopt the most orthodox form of his religious heritage. Orthodoxy alone has shown effective resistance to Nazi nihilism."

James Luther Adams applied that critique in a much less dramatic and more homely way to one Unitarian Universalist parish whose application for membership reads:

> I wish to join the _____ Church to share its free fellowship and to advance its purposes of liberal worship and service. I understand that, by this act, I am not in any way limiting my freedom either of thought or conscience, nor am I surrendering ideals, convictions, or ways of living which I now value.

The application sounds as if membership in this congregation means nothing spiritually and costs nothing ethically. It is the negative statement of a debilitating individualism, not a positive profession of the imperatives of liberal religious faith. This is freedom from, not freedom for, commitment; it implies no sense of promise making or keeping.

Educator Harold Taylor in his study of the Unitarian Universalist movement said, "In a movement where everything is allowed, too little is asserted with passion." In a religious faith that prides itself on theological, political, ethical, and social pluralism, there seems to be no centering purpose that can be shared by all and acted on in the social arena. To agree to disagree, even agreeably, is not an adequate covenant, although this has often been the hallmark of the movement. The reconciliation syndrome is dominant, seeking the lowest common denominator in theology and in ethics. In a world of power, those groups that cherish political pluralism over the capacity to act will become ineffectual. Political pluralism without some rallying center is too expensive a principle. In our time the ascendance of the Religious Right, with its threat to freedom and justice, ought to convince us that a waffling freedom from commitment makes us irrelevant.

Clearly, there can be no creed, not even a social creed, in this movement. However, there is a need for one or more statements of covenant, of promise making and keeping, regarding the responsibilities of persons and communities to the world. This covenantal statement will have several characteristics distinct to its religious tradition: it will be naturalistic; it will be this-worldly (contemporary history will be its sole arena for action); its eschatology will be open-ended; it will derive from human resources (the commitment of persons and communities of persons to universal humanity, which I have expressed as the Beloved Community). Unitarian Universalist theologian Gene Reeves sums it up: "Far from having nothing to say, religious liberals have to proclaim, over and over again, against both religious and secular adversaries, the good news that the future remains open and the Fates are not in control."

James Luther Adams has been a sharp critic of this lack of commitment and discipline in the liberal faith. In his essay "The Place of Discipline in Christian Ethics," he wrote,

> This element of commitment, of change of hearts, of decision, so much emphasized in the Gospels, has been neglected by religious liberalism, and that is the prime source of its enfeeblement. We liberals are largely an uncommitted and therefore a self-frustrating people. Out first task, then, is to restore to liberalism its own dynamic and its own prophetic genius. We

need conversion within ourselves. . . . A holy community must be a militant community with its own explicit faith; and this explicit faith cannot be engendered without disciplines that shape the ethos of the group and that issue in the criticism of the society and of the "religious" community itself.

With this ethical formulation in mind, I suggest the following outline for a Unitarian Universalist social responsibility covenant:

1. We become human beings by making promises and keeping commitments. A Unitarian Universalist needs to do more than sign a membership book; members should be encouraged to explore the disciplines of freedom that issue in some form of explicit faith and ethic. Creedlessness does not imply absence of belief. It implies personal responsibility to formulate a credo, one that has both social implications and responsibilities in a community of faith. We are covenanting creatures.

2. Our covenant is a covenant with all being, with creative, sustaining, transforming powers, interpreted theistically or humanistically. It is living in gratitude that generates responsibility. Its focus is both human beings and the natural environment. We are utterly dependent on our natural environment, grateful recipients of our historic traditions, and cocreators of the future of the planet.

3. Our covenant is both individual and social. We are responsible not only for individual behavior, but also for the character of the society and the preservation of nature. Such a covenant will involve individuals as moral agents, responsible selves, in their interaction with other selves and the world. But the autonomous individual is also a member of the community, a religious community devoted to interests that transcend the self and the group, a community that encompasses humanity and the natural environment.

4. Our covenant is especially directed toward the deprived and the powerless. St. Ambrose, an early church father, suggests this is no new thrust theologically. Speaking directly to the rich, he wrote, "You are not making a gift of your possessions to the poor person. You are handing over to him what is his. For what has been given in common for the use of all, you have arrogated to yourself. The world is given to all and not only to the rich."

5. Good fortune obligates. This is one of the corollaries of reverence for life. Interpreting Schweitzer, ethicist Herbert Spiegelberg con-

tends that we ought not take the blessings of life for granted but should see them as both opportunity and obligation to serve those deprived of them. This is not the principle of *noblesse oblige* (of one well born, great things are expected), a maxim of class ethics that we have seen in Unitarian Universalist history. Schweitzer saw this corollary as applying to everyone who is endowed with natural or circumstantial gifts of life. This principle might be called *bonheur oblige,* or "good fortune obligates," as Spiegelberg has it. "At some point we have to make up to some of the deprived for unearned benefits. . . . The more fortunate are to those less fortunate a compensation in proportion to their handicaps." Schweitzer once said that "the good fortune which we encounter in life should not be taken for granted, but, as a recognition of our gratitude, should be used in some way or other to help render service to others. . . . What share of that good fortune, of which you have received more than others, should you be allowed to keep for yourself?"

This is not an argument for charity, but for justice. It does not involve the giving of alms, but helping to empower the powerless. This dimension of the covenant will be especially difficult for a primarily middle-class denomination. Can the possession of good fortune be justified in a world noted for its chasm between the rich and the poor? Will a group in power share that power with the powerless—or even relinquish it? While definitive answers to these questions are beyond the scope of the present discussion, the prophetic imperative requires at least the sharing of power and the special responsibility of the powerful for the powerless.

A Unitarian Universalist covenant for social responsibility recognizes the nature of its constituency, largely upper middle class. This constituency is perhaps uniquely open to the questions raised above and to other questions about human meaning in a technological society, because its value pattern is not middle class, but far more ethically, socially, and politically progressive than the American middle class as a whole. This constituency is perhaps uniquely able to make decisions affecting many, to help in empowering the powerless. This is the peculiar *bonheur oblige* of a group of people singularly favored by a modern society that dehumanizes millions daily at the same time. The liberal religious community must come to see itself as a surrogate for the powerless. As James Luther Adams put it, "Blessed are the powerful. Blessed are the powerful who acknowledge that their power is a gift that imposes ever new responsibilities and offers ever new though costing joys. Blessed are the powerful who acknowledge that authentic power is the capacity to respond to the covenant, the capacity to secure the performance of binding obligations."

Theologian William Jones calls for a "theology of relinquishment," a deliberate effort to share power and wealth with the poor and powerless, not through charity, but through private and public policies that empower them. The Reverend Fred Muir details a liberation theology for Unitarian Universalists. Such a theology attempts to see history from below, empathetically taking the viewpoint of the powerless. Such a theology begins its work not in theory, but in real-life situations in which the values of one's faith are applied and tested in a continuing praxis, the "dynamic interrelationship between action and theory." The heart of such a faith is the unsparing critique of the *status quo* in terms of justice. Our mandate is to act on behalf of the poor and oppressed, and in so doing we choose "to work for the life-giving and life-sustaining power of the Cosmos," says Muir.

6. A final dimension of a Unitarian Universalist covenant is the need for the renewal of the concept of vocation. Vocation is here understood not simply as our moral responsibilities in our professions, but more fundamentally as human beings. People are called in whatever they do to be responsible for others, to humanity.

Dietrich Bonhoffer illustrated the point well in his essay "The Structure of Responsible Life":

> If, for example, I am a physician, then in the concrete instance I serve not only my patients but also medical science and with it science and the knowledge of truth in general. Although in practice I perform this service at my concrete position, for example at the bedside of a patient, yet I am consciously aware of my responsibility for the whole, and it is only in this that I fulfill my calling. Furthermore, it may happen that I, as a physician, am obliged to recognize and fulfill my concrete responsibility no longer by the sick-bed but, for example, in taking public action against some measure which constitutes a threat to medical science or to human life or to science as such. Vocation is responsibility and responsibility is a total response of the whole man to the whole of reality; for this very reason there can be no petty and pedantic restricting of one's interests to one's professional duties in the narrowest sense.

The Prophetic Covenant

Harold Taylor summarized the role of the Unitarian Universalist movement in his report on theological education many years ago; however, it is still a relevant charge: "Among the denominations, the role of the liberal church is to act at the front edge of intellectual, spiritual and social change in the American religious community and deliberately to engage itself with the elements and forces of contemporary society at the places where these are to be found at their highest tension."

Liberal religion in its Unitarian Universalist form, then, is that prophetic community of free and disciplined men and women working toward the Beloved Community.

Elie Wiesel prompts us along the way with a Hasidic story:

A disciple made the following remark in front of Rebbe Menahkem-Mendl of Kotzk:

"God, who is perfect, took six days to create a world that is not. How is that possible?"

The Rebbe scolded him: "Could you have done better?"

"Yes, I think so," stammered the disciple, who no longer knew what he was saying.

"You could have done better?" the Master cried out. "Then what are you waiting for? You don't have a minute to waste. Go ahead, start working!"

SOCIAL GOSPEL IN PRACTICE

Chapter Six

In Defense of Church "Interference" in Society

Picture this cartoon: a cathedral-sized sanctuary with five people dispersed in an ocean of pews. Up front is the minister preaching: "Political parties need to know that they ignore the churches' statements on social justice at their own risk."

The issue of the church in politics is an old one. The role of the Unitarian Universalist church in the civil rights and the antiwar movements of the sixties and seventies was indisputable. Our work in opposing sexism and homophobia in the eighties and nineties was equally compelling. At the same time we have experienced the emergence of the religious and political Right, symbolized by the Christian Coalition, as a potent political force. It is beyond debate that organized religion tampers with political life; we might even say that it interferes with the politics of the culture. As theologian Emil Brunner states it, "The church exists for mission the way a fire exists for burning."

Voluntary Associations as Service Agencies and as Political Actors

But what is that mission? The church as a voluntary association in American society is increasingly called on to provide what have until recently been public services. As the United States experiences increasing devolution of human services, we find that not only do such services devolve from federal to state government, but also from the public sector to the private sector. Of course, some private organizations like Catholic Charities and the Salvation Army have long accepted government funds, but with strict church–state separation guidelines.

In this time of retrenchment there is an increasing tendency to let the private sector, predominantly religious organizations, handle human needs. It makes powerful rhetoric, but a reality check reveals it to be either a naive hope or a political sham. There are nearly 35 million poor people and millions more near the poverty line in the United States, and some 350,000 religious groups—churches, synagogues, mosques, temples, and similar institutions. This would mean that every one of these groups would, on average, be responsible for well over one hundred poor people, presumably income maintenance, health care, child care, moral support, and the rest. But many of these groups have fewer than one hundred members; most are hard put to meet current expenses to survive; charitable giving is inadequate, and three-fourths of these groups are already involved in community service. Organized religion taking over social welfare is a cruel political joke.

There are other problems with faith-based organizations and "charitable choice," a little-known feature of 1996 welfare reform legislation enabling public funds to be funneled to religious groups. But who would administer this vast network of private sector groups? Who would set policy? Would antiabortion groups take only the chaste? Would Christian Coalition congregations serve gay, lesbian, bisexual, and transgender people? Would poor people of color be served by racist congregations? The private sector is simply not equipped to handle this vast welfare system. And what about the constitutional questions of separation of church and state? Would there be indoctrination of those accepted in programs? What constitutes indoctrination? How make these private religious groups accountable without the intrusive hand of government examining their books? And what about religious orientation as a condition for employment?

There is a basic irony in this faith-based approach. On the one hand, many believe it is because religious groups use their faith resources that they are so effective. On the other hand, it is claimed that religious proselytizing with public funds would be wrong. We cannot have it both ways. Such funding could undermine religious missions by entanglement with government; could prompt bureaucrats to favor certain faiths, especially those who predominate in a given region; and, perhaps most important, lead to reductions in government services. At an April 2000 symposium at Harvard University's Kennedy School of Government, former congressman and Roman Catholic priest Father Richard Drinan said, "Deep down, I have the feeling that this is a cop-out by the government. Government should be doing this [rather than] pushing it onto the churches."

Should religious groups do more? Of course. I suggest, however, there are other roles for the religious community than trying to deliver human services to poor Americans. There is, of course, a service role. While public funds today provide far more assistance than private funds, there is need for nonprofit groups to mend the holes in the fast-disappearing safety net. But even now charities receive roughly one-third of their budgets from government sources, most with careful church–state separation guidelines. The privatizers appear not to understand the distinction between government and religious community responsibilities and capabilities. Religious groups at best provide only a tattered patchwork of services.

Religious groups have a vital role to perform in educating the community about public needs and moral obligation. For example, it might be helpful to study evaluations of current governmental programs instead of today's political correctness that good government is an oxymoron. Eliminating programs, ending welfare as we know it, is not the same as ending poverty. We should debunk the limited perspective of those who, having only a hammer, see every problem as a nail. We need to learn that government programs reduce poverty at a rate five or six times faster than do rates of economic growth; that a rising tide always does lift yachts, but not all boats. We might also learn the golden rule of American politics: Those who have the gold make the rules.

Organized religion must witness to the moral evil of consigning our nation's poor, and especially its children, to the human scrap heap. During the Depression this nation placed an economic floor under its poorest children; now, with "welfare reform" in a $7 trillion economy awash with projected federal government surpluses, we are told we cannot afford to end poverty in the midst of plenty. In fact, no one even talks of ending poverty.

Finally, religious groups must advocate for the powerless in the halls of power. People of religious faith must question the vast and increasing discrepancy between rich and poor, which leaves one in five of our children in poverty while the top fifth of the population realizes unprecedented prosperity. Religious groups should not be seduced by those who would undermine government responsibility for "the general welfare" (Preamble to the U.S. Constitution) by a naive and disingenuous privatization of welfare and related human services. Welfare reform almost always means welfare cuts. And cutting programs is not the same as reforming them. Improvement surely is needed, but not at the price of abdicating our common responsibility for those who have lost in the battleground that the American marketplace has become. Today's politicians are making war on the poor, not on poverty. Too many of us are joining them. It may be that the epitaph of our generation will be "Born citizens—died taxpayers."

And so, as valuable as the direct services of voluntary agencies like churches are, they are still decidedly secondary to the role of the voluntary sector as an independent advocate and critic. In fact, it can be argued that the primary role of voluntary associations in American life is to help shape the vision of a more just social order, to propose programs leading to that vision, to advocate for them with other contenders in the public arena, and to mobilize resources for their adoption and implementation. In our understandable preoccupation with the need for services, we have ignored what is happening in the critical arena of advocacy and criticism. After all, in our tradition, it was Theodore Parker, Dorothy Dix, John Haynes Holmes, and Susan B. Anthony whose controversial efforts paved the way for the great reforms in our history.

And so, paradoxically, the religious community is being asked to take on what have been governmental responsibilities as the market creates casualties that allow some to prosper at the same time that it impoverishes others. Given limited resources, this means that the religious voluntary associations are being increasingly consumed in creating a safety net abandoned by the public sector. Sadly, this is happening at a time when democracy is undermined by public apathy and desperately needs the prophetic voice.

While there is always a place for service, it would seem that the church fulfills its social role more by being a critic and an advocate than by direct service, a function that can be performed more effectively by government and other organizations more suited to the purpose. The prophetic church will call into question the failure of the appropriate groups to deliver the services that it does not have the resources to deliver itself. My contention is that the church, as a voluntary association, should help to shape and implement the vision of the Beloved Community. The free church (Unitarian Universalist in this instance) is an example of a voluntary association, a group of persons who freely unite to pursue certain mutual goals in the public realm.

NATURE OF THE VOLUNTARY ASSOCIATION

Voluntary associations are essentially nonprofit groups that people join deliberately. They are organized around common interests or purposes. There is an agreement, in the case of religion a covenant, to act together to meet the needs of the group and the larger society.

This understanding of voluntary associations presupposes a prophetic view of history that is dynamic and open-ended rather than deterministic. It postulates that people are capable of actively transforming history, rather than being merely passive spectators of historical change, that history does not simply evolve but is determined by conscious decisions and deliberate action. People are empowered for this task by their participation in various associations that promote particular interests. History, then, is understood as the narrative of these various associations interfacing with the larger society. Democracy is neither a consumer good nor a spectator sport.

Voluntary associations are rooted in a conception of human freedom. Freedom is not simply an individualistic value. It is bound up with the freedom of other individuals. Defining freedom is itself a social process in which there is both private space to be and public space to share. This freedom requires that people must have economic resources as well as political rights, which enable them to make choices about their own lives and the common life of the society. If freedom is to be realized, the individual must have real, not merely theoretical, choices. While, for example, political democracy cherishes the "one person–one vote" concept, the structure of campaign financing leads one to believe that the reality is "one dollar–one vote," so pervasive is money in the electoral process. No one believes a billionaire and a pauper have equal freedom in terms of the actual choices open to them.

Such freedom requires an institutional framework. If history is the story of the struggle for freedom, it is not the story of individuals *per se*, but of groups that shape the history. History can be seen as the struggle for freedom from oppressive institutions as freedom-creating institutions confront them. This freedom must be institutionalized if it is not to be subject to the whim and caprice of a ruling elite. For the individual, this means involvement in groups dealing with other institutions. As James Luther Adams says, "By their groups shall ye know them."

Freedom, then, in this sense, is not the opposite of oppression. It is a response to a call, to the prophetic imperative. The appropriate response is participation in a creative process that makes for a just social order.

This conception of freedom provides a basis for the creative transformation of society informed by transcendent norms, not merely freedom from oppressive institutions. We are social creatures, associational beings. For virtually all our needs, cooperation with others is required, resulting in the creation of communities. Some communities are involuntary: the family, for instance, is a natural community about which choice is somewhat limited. We also do not usually choose the national association in which we live. Voluntary associations, by contrast, are human groupings, which are a function of human freedom. In this sense, voluntary associations are unique to the democratic form of government. The voluntary principle affirms the freedom of the individual and the group. Social decisions are made on the basis of democratic persuasion, not arbitrary coercion. Such groups exercise power through organization and make possible an ongoing process of peaceful change, what Adams calls the "institutional gradualization of revolution."

BRIEF HISTORY OF THE VOLUNTARY ASSOCIATION

The beginnings of the voluntary association can be traced to the primitive Christian church, in which small groups met voluntarily for worship and service, often in defiance of the state. As Christianity became the religion of the empire, this dimension of the church's existence became vestigial. These small Christian groups next emerge at the time of the Reformation, especially as seen in the left wing of the Reformation. These groups were heretical. However, this is a word of praise, not blame, because the literal meaning of heresy is from the Greek *harein* and means "I choose."

The Anabaptists, the full-way or radical reformers, are but one example of these heretical groups. Theirs was a chosen community for the salvation of all baptized members, marked by asceticism, pacifism, liberty, toleration, and the separation of church and state. Its central feature was the voluntary nature of membership. This phenomenon was the forerunner of what we know as the gathered church, with congregational polity.

Such voluntary associations became an important feature of the American scene in both the secular and religious realms. Benjamin Franklin was prototypical in his founding of voluntary associations: the American Philosophical Association, libraries, societies of learning, an academy for the education of youth in Pennsylvania, the Pennsylvania Hospital, and a society for the abolition of slavery.

James Madison in *The Federalist Papers* discussed the concept of factions extensively. It was his view that the competition of factions would disperse power and thereby prevent its concentration in any single group. He contended that there should be a "separation of powers" in the Constitution so as to institutionalize this balance of contending forces. Political parties developed out of this application of voluntarism to political life.

In nineteenth-century America, such groups proliferated in the heady air of freedom. The first systematic treatment of voluntary associations was William Ellery Channing's 1825 report to the American Unitarian Association, "Remarks on Associations." Another observer, Alexis de Tocqueville, said in his *Democracy in America*, "In no country in the world has the principle of association been more successfully used, or applied to a greater multitude of objects, than in America. . . . Wherever at the head of some new undertaking you see the government in France or a man of rank in England, in the United States, you will be sure to find an association." De Tocqueville can be summarized here as saying that wherever two or three Americans are gathered together it is likely that a committee is being formed.

As American society in the twentieth century has become increasingly complex, there has been a continual proliferation of such groups. This variety of human enterprises has been scoffed at by many who criticize the busy-ness of American life. However, the collapse of such civic participation in Nazi Germany indicates the power and importance of what have sometimes been called intermediate groups, which stand between the individual and the increasingly totalitarian state in which there are no countervailing sources of power.

One of the most detailed political analyses of this particular problem is found in William Kornhauser's *The Politics of Mass Society*. In contrasting liberal democracy and totalitarianism, he concluded that the essential reason why democratic freedom has survived mass society is that a democracy thrives in a pluralistic model that has created a number of effective voluntary groups. These groups serve as intermediaries between the people and the government. They protect the elite from the masses by giving vent to emotions and protest and channeling both into creative, peaceful, and effective activities. This channeling preserves the autonomy of the elite to govern without fear of mass revolt. At the same time, intermediate groups, through their own political power, protect the masses from arbitrary governmental restraint of liberty. They do this by organizing groups of citizens and giving a focus for protest and participation in decision making. This prevents the atomization of the people, while providing a broad dispersal of power.

In Nazi Germany and Fascist Italy, for example, there were few, if any, effective intermediate groups. The elite were able to manipulate and mobilize the atomized and alienated masses for their own aggrandizement. The elite simply moved into the power vacuum created by the absence of viable voluntary associations. Kornhauser concluded that there are two necessary and sufficient conditions for the survival of liberal democracy: (1) There must be extensive self-government, private as well as public, and individuals must belong to several self-governing units; and (2) there must be extensive opportunities for elites to formulate policies and take action without *ad hoc* interference from the outside by an unorganized mass. Thus social pluralism is the best guarantee of democracy.

More recently in American history, the voluntary association has had significant social–political impact. The Civil Rights movement, which was able to launch a powerful, if unfinished, revolution in American race relations, was largely spearheaded by voluntary citizen groups, most notably religious institutions. The National Association for the Advancement of Colored People brought the suit that resulted in the historic *Brown v. Board of Education* decision on desegregation in 1954. Martin Luther King, Jr., came to prominence first through the Montgomery Improvement Association and later the Southern Christian Leadership Conference. It is generally accepted that the religious lobby pushed civil rights bills through the Congress in the wake of the 1963 March on Washington. The antiwar movement of the sixties and seventies, much of it centered in religious communities, can be said to have hastened the end of the Vietnam War. It was the constant pressure of citizen groups such as the American Civil Liberties Union and various *ad hoc* organizations that kept the impeachment issue alive until, under threat of impeachment, President Richard Nixon resigned. Good government groups like Common Cause and Public Citizen are watchdogs on the workings of the federal government. Furthermore, it is generally acknowledged that it was liberal religious groups that prompted attacks on sweat-shop labor and on the developed nations to consider debt forgiveness to Third World nations. The environmental movement for eco-justice, a balancing of stewardship for Earth and economic development, has important allies in faith communities at all levels.

We can summarize the history of voluntary associations by saying that they originally grew out of the religious impulse, basically the left wing of the Protestant Reformation. Beginning as a religious heresy, the principle of dissent was secularized and politicized to become the foundation of modern pluralistic democracy. Now these groups have a more than ever indispensable role in the shaping of a responsible society.

THE VOLUNTARY ASSOCIATION: A TYPOLOGY

We can categorize voluntary associations and apply them to the religious community in one of six ways: (1) by motivation, (2) by goal, (3) by duration, (4) by geography, (5) by focus, or (6) by source of authority.

By Motivation

Are they public or self-interest (expressive) groups? The church does not fit neatly into any of these categories: it is both self- and public interested, clearly expressive in some of its functions, providing an outlet for individuals to engage in self-actualization. It is also instrumental to the extent that it participates in advocating and effecting social change. Hence the church embodies both self- and public interest and in a single community combines persons who have joined for these and, as we shall see, other purposes.

By Goal

Do they aim at instrumental systemic change or are they intent on service, basically accepting the current structure of things? The church has traditionally been service-oriented, a charitable organization. Now, however, it can be seen to be interested in public policy, often in terms of systemic change. Church involvement in the Civil Rights, antipoverty, antiwar, environmental, and human rights movements suggests an extension beyond a purely service orientation.

By Duration

Are they spontaneous, *ad hoc,* or do they have an ongoing existence? The church, unlike many voluntary associations, is extensive over time; its life does not depend on the duration of a single cause or issue. It is multifaceted in terms of interest and sustains itself institutionally when other groups fall by the wayside. Therefore, one of its weaknesses, its multifaceted nature, is also one of its strengths.

By Geography

What do they consider their sphere of responsibility? The local congregation usually takes the geographical spread of its members, a metropolitan area, or a neighborhood, as its turf. This expands with the grouping of congregations into districts, dioceses, national denominations, and finally international bodies (the World Council of Churches—Protestant, the International Association of Religious Freedom, or the Global Network of Unitarian Universalists). Ultimately, the world is the arena of religious responsibility.

By Focus

What publics do voluntary associations aim to influence? The church, first and foremost, focuses on its own constituency, seeking to help people live out their professed values. Then the focus may be expanded to those beyond the church (in influencing public opinion) or to decision makers (advocacy and lobbying).

By Source of Authority

From what normative structure do they take guidance? The church claims a transcending authority, God or the equivalent. I have argued here that participation in the process of creativity to seek the Beloved Community is such a transcending norm in the Unitarian Universalist movement. Many groups claim the authority of competence: business, labor, or professional groups. Others claim democratic authority vested in the U.S. Constitution and system of law (ACLU and other secular civil rights and reform groups). Some claim a community mandate (groups lobbying to protect or change zoning laws). In its claim to a transcendent norm, the church identifies itself as a unique voluntary association.

A SOCIAL CONFLICT MODEL: THE INTERFACES OF POWER

The role of the church can best be seen in the context of the interfaces of power groups in a democratic society. The role of the voluntary association is critical. The basic form is the conflict model of society; that is, we take as a given that in a complex democratic society conflict exists between groups. This conflict stems ontologically from the reality that differences between individuals and between groups are part of the order of nature. This is in contradistinction to a model of harmonism, which is based on a faith that an "invisible hand" will automatically harmonize persons and groups seeking their own self-interest. History indicates the failure of that philosophy, the breakdown of capitalism in the U.S. Great Depression being a prime example.

The conflict model of society was developed early in American history in *The Federalist Papers,* particularly in papers 10 and 51 written by James Madison. In Number 10, Madison begins,

> Among the numerous advantages promised by a well-constructed Union, none deserves to be more accurately developed than its tendency to break and control the violence of faction . . . a number of citizens, whether they amount to a majority or minority of the whole, who are united and actuated by some common impulse of passion, or of interest, adverse to the rights of other citizens, or to the permanent and aggregate interests of the community. . . . As long as the reason

of man continues fallible, and he is at liberty to exercise it, different opinions will be formed. . . . The latent causes of faction are thus sown in the nature of man.

Madison's faith was in the dynamic interaction of the various factions in which no one would gain hegemony, but each would be a check on every other. Hence we must accept pluralism, the conflict model of society, and the "dissensus" within it, not as a necessary evil, but as a value in itself. Better a true conflict of interest with a commonly accepted set of ground rules for dissensus, consensus, and decision making than a false harmonism that is either structurally impossible or the result of hegemony of one totalistic institution, either the state or private economic power.

In such a conflict model of society the fundamental relationship between factions is power, the capacity to participate in the shaping of social decisions. It is the capacity to achieve goals, to exercise influence, to affect policy. The current scene suggests that the voluntary association is in some difficulty, with the rising power of both public governments and those "private governments" that have become prominent in the public sphere, especially economic institutions. The corporate merger mania of the eighties and the nineties is a case in point.

The task of the voluntary association is to make both the public sector of government and the private sector of the economy accountable. It must expose the overwhelming power of the economic sector over the political sector. It must make both accountable to the larger interests of the people. Government can then be used to represent a public that is at the mercy of the competitive marketplace. Abraham Lincoln said that government should do for the people what they cannot do, or do so well, for themselves.

What, then, is the distinctive function of the religious community as a voluntary association in a conflict model of society? The religious community (church, synagogue, mosque, temple, denomination) is a voluntary association in American society and as such wields power. It possesses power—resources of funds, buildings, and personnel that are used for a variety of purposes, at least one of which is to influence the society, if only to preserve the self-interest of the religious community itself. For example, we can scarcely conceive of any religious institution that would not become political if its tax-exempt status were threatened.

However, the religious community differs somewhat from other voluntary associations in that the source of its authority is not the community or the state. It claims transcendent sources of authority.

Therefore, it can bring a fresh perspective to the community of dialogue. Yet the church in general has been hesitant to speak such a word. One possible reason for this is a basic misunderstanding of the constitutional idea of separation of church and state. This problem is well stated by Karl Herz as he discusses "The Nature of Voluntary Associations" in *Voluntary Associations: A Study of Groups in Free Societies*:

> [T]he ideological use of the separation doctrine—whether of the religious from the political, or the political from the economic—misses the essence of the American tradition: the American protest is against unilateral structural control of the one sphere of life by another, against totalitarianism of the right or the left. The maintenance of structural independence is a condition of freedom; the maintenance of vital relationships is equally a condition of meaningful freedom.

In *The Culture of Disbelief*, Stephen Carter argues for the vigorous participation of the religious community in public debate. He believes that a false and overly strict concept of church–state separation has actually had the unintended effect of stifling the religious view. While he does not often agree with the policy prescriptions of the Religious Right, he welcomes them to the community of the dialogue and believes they should have their day in court.

Thus the separation of church and state does not intend to nullify religious influence on social policy. Rather, it is the attempt, based on historical experience, to prevent any one social institution from gaining hegemony at the expense of others. Separation of church and state does not mean the separation of religion and politics. Quite the contrary. Separation of church and state is the necessary social arrangement that facilitates the interaction of the religious community, as one among many associations, with the state. The church, not being dependent for its existence on government, is free to speak to the state, critically if necessary, in the light of its norms and values. The religious association has no special privileges in this interaction, but it does have the same rights and prerogatives as any other voluntary association. Not to speak publicly, not to engage in the political sphere, would be to create a power vacuum into which other groups with or without a transcending vision would step. Thus, the religious community, as a voluntary association, not only has a right but an obligation to engage in the struggles of a pluralistic society.

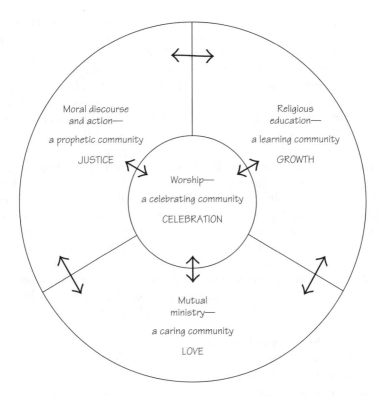

Model of the Unitarian Universalist Congregation

THE UNITARIAN UNIVERSALIST CHURCH AS A VOLUNTARY ASSOCIATION

The prophetic imperative of the Unitarian Universalist church grows organically out of a doctrine of the liberal church. The above figure illustrates this doctrine of the liberal church (Unitarian Universalist) and demonstrates how the various dimensions interact. My focus here is on how the church as a community of moral discourse and social action is informed and supported by the others.

Worshipping Community

Imagine a circle within a circle. The center circle is worship, the celebration of the value experiences of life. Out of this spiritual center grows what we think and do as individuals and as a community. Our

connectedness with cosmos, world, history, and each other is con-
firmed and celebrated here. This is what James Luther Adams calls
"centerstance in the midst of circumstance."

The church is a worshipping community, a religious community
that deliberately and regularly gathers together to celebrate life in all
its dimensions. Worship understood as the celebration of life is the
most generally accepted definition in Unitarian Universalist circles
today. Worship derives from the Anglo-Saxon *weorthscipe,* pointing to
and celebrating that which is of worth. Religion is derived from the
Latin *religare* and means to bind together. The form of this religious
worship is called a liturgy from the Greek words *laos* (people) and
ergos (work), literally, "the people's work." All this leads to an understanding of worship as a binding together or coming together of people to fashion ceremonies pointing to what they regard as of worth.

While the act of worship is in itself a religious activity of intrinsic
worth, it is also instrumental in motivating and sustaining human
efforts in serving the mandates of the prophetic imperative. It serves to
strengthen and maintain commitment to social change by pointing to
justice, freedom, equality, and the Beloved Community as ends to be
sought.

I refer here not only to formal worship in church sanctuary and
church school, but to informal experiences by which transcendent values break through the ordinary and move us to reconstruct our experiences, raising up symbols of our loftiest ideals. Here we measure
ourselves against the best we know—try to get what has been called
"a God's eye view of ourselves," as religious educator and theologian
Angus H. MacLean puts it in *The Wind in Both Ears.*

The prophet Amos gave the most devastating critique of worship
not in the service of justice: "I hate, I despise your feasts, and take no
delight in your solemn assemblies . . . but let justice roll down like
waters, and righteousness like an ever-flowing stream" (Amos
5:21–24).

I do not understand corporate worship as simply one more means
to rev up the troops for social change. Worship has many purposes,
both personal and corporate. But if worship does not embody commitment to the Beloved Community, I take no delight in it. Somewhere
between "playing church with bells and smells" and a political action
meeting is the worshipping community nourishing itself for the work
of the world. At its best, worship is an expression of, but not a substitute for, social responsibility. The religious life of the community in
worship overflows into public ministry.

Caring Community

The second circle circumscribes three equal segments: in one is mutual ministry, a caring community in which we nourish one another despite our political and social differences, bind up the wounds of our defeats, and share our joys, both personal and social.

This caring community is a response of the church to the ultimate loneliness of the individual in a mass society and in an indifferent cosmos. It is a religious community in which there is a mutual ministry of persons based on *agape* (love). It is a corollary of Luther's concept of "the priesthood of all believers," that each member of the religious community should be a priest to all others. It is the Beloved Community in miniature. The caring community internal to the church is based on person-to-person, face-to-face, I–thou relationships. However, the same reverence for life that issues in this kind of personal relationship also undergirds a broader sense of the caring community that embraces people beyond the range of immediate personal experience.

The church as a caring community and the church as a social change agent may seem contradictory and in competition, but these facets of the church are complementary. Every personal problem is also a social problem, and every social problem is also a personal problem. The current corporate practice of downsizing is a predominant factor in economic life. While it is more often viewed as a social problem, the individuals who lose their jobs must sell their homes and move from friends and family. Those whose retirement is in jeopardy find it very much a personal problem.

The caring community and prophetic community of the church touch in sensitive ways. In the fall of 1983, the First Unitarian Church of Rochester, New York, voted by 156 to 1 to endorse the nuclear freeze, by secret ballot. However, we all knew who the one was; she was a dear lady and a staunch Reagan–Bush conservative on such issues. It was clear that she needed a ministry from all of us who loved her, but also loved the freeze. I wrote this column for her and for us:

> Note to a minority of one: congregational democracy can be a difficult process. While the majority have reason to feel good about the resolution supporting the nuclear freeze, this note is directed to the minority of one who opposed it. It takes courage to vote one's convictions when it is clear one is going to be a small minority. Yet it is crucial to the process that this voice be heard. The minority, even of one, reminds the major-

ity that conscience counts for something in liberal religion. That one vote reminds us of our essential pluralism on many difficult issues of religion and politics. That voice helps keep the majority from becoming arrogant and self-righteous. We needed that vote for the good of us all.

Community of Religious Education

The second section of the outer circle represents a corollary of the priesthood of all believers: the church as an educational community, a life-span learning community. I refer not only to what happens in the church school for one or two hours Sunday morning or during a weekly adult education class, but to the totality of potential learning experiences for people of all ages.

In a church community without creed or dogma, or even explicit articulation of faith by consensus, the priesthood of all believers is a radical reality. The church exists as an educational community providing the resources in history, theology, philosophy, and ethics for the individual to create a working faith, in freedom. Religious education in the liberal church is a life-span process of developing a core of meanings and values to which to commit our lives.

This educational community is not solely a vehicle for personal growth, however; it has social implications as well. Harold Taylor, in his study of the Unitarian Universalist movement, *A Plan of Action for the UU Ministry*, sees education as an instrument of social action. He furthermore notes how essential education is in creating value in a creedless church. This goes beyond merely transferring a heritage from generation to generation.

> But the liberal church by its nature must think of education in much broader terms—as the process by which religious values themselves are recreated by the continued infusion of fresh thinking and new ideas from the sources of contemporary knowledge and culture. Otherwise it has no place from which to draw its own spiritual nourishment and sustenance, being itself an enterprise devoted to extending the frontier of religious discovery.

COMMUNITY OF MORAL DISCOURSE AND ACTION

In the third segment of the outer circle is the church as a community of moral discourse and action. By this I mean that at every age level there should be an ongoing conversation about moral values and social action. Such a conversation can neither be indoctrinating nor neutral in tone. Nothing would be further from such moral discourse than to make our churches sociopolitical propaganda stations for the latest liberal social action fad. The church must seek to penetrate the political order with justice, but not itself be co-opted by the platform of any political party.

I do not suggest that social responsibility is, or ought to be, the central thrust of the liberal church. Neither social responsibility nor private meditation exhausts the religious experience. What I do claim is that liberal religion cannot exist significantly in the absence of either. Social responsibility without personal spiritual growth, without informed ethical analysis, becomes "do-goodism" of the worst kind. Spiritual nurture without a social component becomes privatized, demonic.

If partisan politics is unworthy of this moral discourse, so too is neutrality. According to tradition "Silent Cal" Coolidge returned from church one Sunday morning. His wife asked him where he had been.

"To church," he replied.

"What did the minister say?"

"He talked about sin."

"And what did he say about sin?"

"He was against it."

As preacher and teacher, I do not feel bound to talk about sin only in the abstract. I expect to name it as I see it. I expect an open mind, respect for various viewpoints, but I also expect commitments. To refuse to honor those commitments under the guise of neutrality is not good education. It reminds me of the story of a mother and child talking about a picture in which Martian creatures are devouring spaceship earthlings. "Is that right?" asked the child. "Do Unitarian Universalists believe in that?" She replied in good liberal fashion: "Some believe in it, some do not, and some are not ready to make up their minds." In justice work we do not have the option of continuous postponement; conviction and action are required.

Moral discourse is carried on in pew and pulpit, in classroom and coffee hour, in office and seminar. It draws on the historical "for instances" of moral and ethical reflection and behavior. It delineates a moral tradition or traditions in which we stand. It transcends purely partisan rhetoric. It links religious values with "middle axioms" and policy choices.

Take, for example, my experience in an adult program "Religion in the Market Place." Our initial sessions were a very basic introduction to moral tradition and ethical decision making. Then each member of the group brought in a case study out of personal experience. In case study fashion, we worked through that problem, not necessarily trying to solve it, but suggesting new insights and perspectives. One scientist brought in an issue in which a colleague had made what he thought was an important discovery in health research. The company vice-president was not only not interested because the company did not deal in that area of health care products, but threatened the researcher with loss of job and blackballing if he took his discovery elsewhere. What should he do? The discussion was fascinating and troubling. We had become a community of moral discourse. What remains, of course, is translating this moral discourse into social action.

The point to be made with regard to this doctrine of the liberal church and advocacy is this: Social action is not the central function of the church. It is a vital function, but it must emerge out of a religious community that serves well the functions of worship, caring, and education. Yet a church that ignores this function fails to understand its mandate to seek the Beloved Community. Social action is a necessary but not sufficient dimension for a Unitarian Universalist church.

If I have described this circle within a circle correctly, you will notice that each section touches every other section (the arrows between them in both directions suggest their interpenetration). They are understood not as administrative categories, but as dimensions, functions of the church occurring at many programmatic places. This is a model of the prophetic church. This church teaches by what it says and by what it does. It is quadraphonic, not monaural sound.

A RATIONALE FOR INTERFERENCE

In response to a layperson's query as to whether voting resolutions on matters of public policy by religious institutions constituted a violation of the principle of separation of church and state, James Luther Adams wrote an essay entitled "On Interference." What follows is a formal rationale for the "interference" of the liberal church in the social world of power built on this discussion of the liberal church as a voluntary association.

The first argument is from history. Historically, Unitarian Universalism, a theological heresy, has also been a social heresy. From its beginnings in the left wing of the Reformation to the Unitarian Universalist Association's Beacon Press's publication of the *Pentagon Papers*, there has been a strong pattern of retaining personal and institutional freedom to criticize government and to participate in social decisions. From Michael Servetus's refusing to repudiate his antitrinitarianism in Calvin's Genevan theocracy to Michael Ferber's refusal to be drafted during the Vietnam War, there has been a staunch defense of freedom from governmental oppression. Such protests have never represented the unanimous opinion among Unitarian Universalists, but, in the main, this kind of heresy has been defended. If we are to "merit the wind we inherit," be active recipients of this prophetic tradition, we will need to act under its mandate.

A second argument for interference is that religion possesses both vertical (transcendent) and horizontal (ethical and social) dimensions. We recall Channing's assertion that "religion is a social principle." Ralph Waldo Emerson also expressed it in his 1870 essay "Society and Solitude": "Solitude [alone] is impracticable, and society [alone] is fatal. . . . We must keep our head in the one and our hands in the other. The conditions are met, if we keep our independence [our private lives] yet do not lose our sympathy [our public lives]. . . . These wonderful horses need to be driven by fine hands."

Here again we may find the concept of vocation helpful. While it has come to be understood in our day as related exclusively to the way in which a person earns a living, in its original sense it referred to the responsibility of the individual to respond to God's action on us. It assumed a responsibility to the social world of which the individual was a part.

A third reason for interference is the pragmatic theory of meaning. Briefly stated, this theory says that ideas have consequences. Social beliefs are of no consequence unless they are somehow embodied in associations that can exert power in the public realm. Here there is great ambiguity in liberal religious circles as we find a religious people with a strong convergence toward progressive views on most social questions, but who seem unable to make these views manifest with power. The tension between individual autonomy in religion and ethics and institutional expression of these views is dysfunctional.

The contrast of such a liberal religious movement, stressing individual autonomy, with a dogmatic, hierarchically organized religious movement such as Roman Catholicism is striking. Take the issue of abortion, for example, for which both groups have strong but diametrically opposed views. Official Roman Catholic teaching condemns abortion in virtually every instance. Unitarian Universalist Association resolutions protecting reproductive freedom have long had overwhelming support at General Assemblies and in congregations. What is striking is not the divergence of views, but the ability of the Roman Catholic faith to mobilize effectively its resources for a strong effort to effect legal prohibition of abortion and the general inability of Unitarian Universalists to do the same for their position. This discrepancy, in my view, cannot be totally explained by the vast differential in the size of the two movements. It has to do with the reticence of liberal religious people to institutionalize their social concern.

The fourth argument for interference is political necessity. As there are no vacuums in nature, so there is no vacuum in the social life of a community. The absence of one center of power from the society will enable another to assert its power more forcefully. Here is revealed a certain political naiveté among Unitarian Universalists ("children of light"), who cling to individual polity and refuse to have their church speak for them. The result, unless there are other power groups to do the speaking, is that no one will speak. The autonomous, isolated, atomized individual has virtually no power in the public realm. To the extent that a liberal religious word needs to be spoken to a conservative religious word, the Unitarian Universalist faith is in danger of being made mute.

It is often argued that secular groups are gathered around each of these issues, and this is true. However, should those of us who wish to be counted as a religious voice in public debate be denied that right? If we have no religious voice on gay rights, for instance, it would be easy to imagine most people believing that most or all religious people oppose gay rights. Orthodox and conservative religious bodies argue against the homosexual lifestyle and "special" rights for gays and lesbians from their religious sources—in this case, a distortion of the Bible. Must we remain silent religiously, allowing only secular bodies to represent our strongly held views in public?

A fifth argument is based on the capacity to act, to exert power in a society. Power implies obligations. Unitarian Universalists are among the elite of American society in terms of socioeconomic status. According to a 1993 study, ninety-five percent had attended college, eighty-three percent graduated, and sixty-five percent had some postgraduate education. Median family income was $50,000, approximately $20,000 above the national median. A large percentage are professionals, managers, or owners. This picture represents a people who are in a position to be exceedingly influential in the society. No doubt more recent studies would yield similar results.

A further advantage accrues to the church as a power center. Unlike many voluntary associations whose life is limited to a given period in which a given cause elicits spontaneous energy, the church is an ongoing institution that is not limited by time or cause. The church has been, is, and most likely will continue to be a factor in the social sphere. This provides a potential constituency unknown in many voluntary associations.

This argument from capacity to act is a result of the principle that "good fortune obligates." The corollary used here is that among those who possess power the obligation is to use it. James Luther Adams reminded us, "Blessed are the powerful who acknowledge that authentic power is the capacity to respond to the covenant, the capacity to secure the performance of binding obligations."

A sixth argument is rooted in the danger of co-optation by the state. What I advocate is a radical conceptualization of the separation of church and state. In a community where so much power is vested in a central authority (government), the church for its own self-interest must resist every temptation to blindly serve that state. The Vietnam War era episode in which the FBI investigated bank records of the Unitarian Universalist Association after publication of the *Pentagon Papers* is a case in point. Without a substantial social thrust that can resist such violation of civil liberties, the independence of the church is in grave danger.

At the turn of the last century, Walter Rauschenbusch saw the tendency of the church to be a captive of the culture. He spoke of "culture Protestantism" wherein the church is more influenced by the nature of the prevailing culture than *vice versa*. Rauschenbusch wrote that "society has always influenced the Church, and . . . the Church when it has dropped to the level of its environment, has simply yielded to the law of social gravitation." If the church does not respond to its transcendent norms, then it will likely become an apologist for the status quo. It will lose its very reason for being, to lift men and women upward toward the Beloved Community.

A final argument for liberal church interference in the larger society is the need for what has been called a conscience constituency. In a society of many power centers, most are self-interest groups, especially the large economic institutions. Few voluntary associations consider and seek the public interest as their central goal. The church, in this case the liberal church, should be able to act from an altruistic frame of reference, minimizing self-interest as a factor. Thus it is able to act on behalf of the powerless. Unless there is a strong conscience constituency, the inequities of power in American society will become even more pervasive. As we know, those who possess power do not voluntarily relinquish it.

According to the foregoing arguments, the liberal church as a voluntary association has not only a right but a mandate to act as a power center, to interfere in the public realm. And, judging from their response to the 1998 *Fulfilling the Promise* survey, most Unitarian Universalists want their church to speak out. In answer to the question "To what extent should your congregation contribute to spreading the UU faith?", the overwhelmingly first-choice answer was "Be outspoken in our community, a voice for justice based on our principles."

FREEDOM OF CONSCIENCE AND ACTION

The foregoing rationale has been challenged by, among others, Unitarian Universalists for Freedom of Conscience, who believe any political action by the local church, district, or denomination is a violation of the Unitarian Universalist right of conscience. The late Paul Beattie argued that "Politics has become religion and religion has become politics." How does one respond to such criticism?

Amos had it easy; so did Isaiah and Jeremiah and Micah, all those Hebrew prophets who were the mouthpieces for God, who believed that Yahweh whispered in their pearly ears. They did not have congregations to which they were accountable. Nor was congregational polity an issue. Nor was freedom of conscience. The only issue for them was justice—or rather injustice.

Unitarian Universalist ministers, while more in danger of their jobs than their lives, don't have it so easy. Most do not claim to speak for God. Most of us speak out of the subterranean depths of our own conscience, to which we are accountable, along with a congregation for which we are responsible.

It was Theodore Parker who formed what was probably the first social action committee for the church militant. In the face of pressing problems, "is the church to say nothing, do nothing?" he asked. Parker believed "the clergy . . . are unconsciously bought up, their speech paid for, or their silence." He ended his vigorous social ministry with a letter to his congregation: "I know I have offended the feelings of many of you, my friends. . . . You never made me your minister merely to flatter or to please, but to instruct and serve."

We do not say, "Your spiritual life is important, but you do not need to attend corporate worship—go into your closet alone and pray"; we do not say, "You ought to be a compassionate, caring person, but do not organize your church to care for your neighbors, do it on your own"; we do not say, "Your religious education is a life-long quest, but do not engage in organized education, do it yourself;" nor should we say, "You are a citizen of a global community for which you are responsible, but do not engage in church social action; go out and do your own thing in the community—and we will cheer you on—maybe."

I wonder if such issues were considered by the Confessing Church of Nazi Germany, which constituted itself a spiritual and political force to oppose Adolf Hitler. How would they have fared if each of them had gone into the world to do their own thing? A collective voice of religion was needed, and the Confessing Church of Bonhoffer and Niemoeller courageously spoke out. And where would South Africa's anti-apartheid movement have been were it not for the church's collective voice in the *Kairos* document? And would we have had a civil rights movement were it not for the organizational thrust of the religious community?

To me the issue is not whether the church should be involved in social action. This cannot be helped. The church lives in a political world as fish swim in the sea. Our location in the community, the groups we allow to use our facilities, the response we make to pleas for help, all compel us to take institutional positions. We cannot avoid them. The church teaches by what it does.

How do we separate ourselves as social advocates from the community of faith? Surely I cannot as a minister. But must I refrain from speaking to public issues out of my faith tradition? Is the church merely a collection of individuals? Or does it have a life that includes, but also transcends, the life of its constituent parts? In the public square we hear a variety of voices, many of them religious. Shall we be mute in this chorus because we are afraid of offending, or shall we risk democracy and take the consequences?

Clearly, the issue will not soon, if ever, be settled. This is the price we pay in a free religious community. Our predicament and our promise are amusingly portrayed by an old story of the minister who was asked to resolve a dispute in the congregation. When one group presented their case, the minister said, "You're right, you're absolutely right!" When the other group presented their case the minister said, "You're right, you're absolutely right!" When the similarity of the replies was noted by a neutral board member, the minister said, "You're right, you're absolutely right!"

CHAPTER SEVEN

Congregational
Mobilization for Justice

In the Gospel according to Matthew, Jesus is reported to have said, "Many are called, but few are chosen" (Matthew 22:14). While Unitarian Universalists are probably not God's chosen people, we have often been called "God's frozen people" for our tendency to be proper rather than passionate, to do a better job discussing social problems than solving them. An observer of nineteenth-century Unitarians put it this way: "They are sensible, plausible, candid, subtle, and original in discussing any social evil or abuse. But somehow they don't get at it!"

Poet Lee Carroll Pieper, thinking no doubt of Jesus' words, "Many are called, but few are chosen," has wryly written: "Many are called but most are frozen in corporate or collective cold; these are the stalled who choose not to be chosen except to be bought and sold." Perhaps Pieper had Unitarian Universalists in mind.

In his "Pagan Sermon," C. Wright Mills offers a scathing and not undeserved indictment of the churches:

> But you may say, "Don't let's get the church into politics." You might well say that with good conscience were the political role of the church to be confined to what it has been and what it is. But in view of what it might be, if you say that you are saying, "Don't let's get the church into the world; let's be another distraction from reality." This world is political. Politics, understood for what it really is today, has to do with the decisions men make which determine how they shall live and how they shall die. They are not living very well, and they are not going to die very well either. Politics is the locale of both evil and of good. If you do not get the church into politics, you cannot confront evil and you cannot work for good.

You will be a subordinate amusement and a political satrap of whatever is going. You will be the great Christian joke.

If the Unitarian Universalist movement is not to be a great Christian joke, we must mobilize for systemic social change. I believe Unitarian Universalists are called to live under the prophetic imperative. How might a local congregation mobilize itself as a prophetic community?

I suggest eight models for social action in the local congregation. This by no means exhausts the possibilities, nor is this the only way they might be developed. They are merely suggestive and intended to stimulate individual congregations to organize in ways appropriate to them. The key is to organize. Don't mourn, organize! Social action at its best involves the total congregation in a conscious effort to fulfill its special role. This happens not by accident or indirection, but by intentional and disciplined activity.

A church may select for implementation one or more of these models, some combination of them, or all of them. The *sine qua non* of social responsibility at the local level is the first model, the church as a community of moral discourse. Without this emphasis, none of the other models will have meaning or possibility. The spirit of this discussion is aptly summarized in a story told about Quaker leader William Penn. After an hour of silence at a Quaker meeting, an obviously frustrated visitor asked Penn, "When does the service begin?" He answered, "Only when the meeting ends."

SOCIAL RESPONSIBILITY MODELS

1. The Church as a Community of Moral Discourse

An old Jewish story tells of a synagogue that had been without a rabbi for some twenty years and was now on the verge of being torn apart by arguments about how to do some of the central prayer rituals. Finally, out of desperation they sent a delegation to the old rabbi, long retired, to inquire what the tradition really was supposed to be. Each side presented its case, denouncing the other side for distorting the true tradition. After they had concluded, the rabbi asked if it was true that each side was sure that its way was right. "Yes," both sides responded. "And both sides seem to think that the other side is deeply mistaken and is about to ruin everything should their view prevail?" asked the rabbi. "Yes," both sides responded, "the other side is going to distort the truth and ruin the community. So what is the tradition?"

The rabbi had no problem: "The state of affairs you describe in our synagogue—*That is the tradition.*"

This may well be the tradition in many of our congregations, but I argue that this moral discourse can be disciplined and made effective for both personal growth and effective social action. The key is to take the normal variety of opinions on social issues and become intentional in transforming them from coffee hour chatter into moral discourse and social action.

This model involves the whole congregation in moral discourse, delineating the church's moral tradition, fundamental principles of ethics, and their application to particular situations. The idea is to permeate the society with members of the congregation as change agents, the silent interpenetration of religious people into the larger society. This concept is central to the church as a social change agent. It informs all that the church might do in other modalities. It assumes that basic religious values are internalized by people and are expressed in social life. It seems clear that religious and moral values do affect social beliefs and actions. In whatever age, it is inescapable that religious convictions do shape social, economic, and policy action. This may happen unconsciously or self-consciously. I argue that Unitarian Universalists ought to seek to sew their religious and social convictions into a seamless garment and that the institution that nurtures their faith and their action must be mobilized to help transform the world.

First, Unitarian Universalists need to understand that we share a rich and extensive moral tradition. Our problem is that too few of us know and understand it. We have been called "Jews without a history." An illustration of the relevance of the comprehension of moral tradition is provided by Unitarian Universalist historian Conrad Wright in his essay "Social Cohesion and the Uses of the Past" as he describes an episode at the May Meetings of the American Unitarian Association some years ago:

> [W]hat happened was that one of our younger ministers, animated by very deep idealism, offered a motion to the effect that the financial aid of the Association should be denied to any member church which did not live up to the moral standards of the Association at large on some issue then being agitated. . . . One could see the delegates getting all set to line up at the microphones to take off on an hour or two of excited and inconclusive discussion of the kind that has become characteristic of such occasions. . . . I had been told more than once of

the loss to our cause because John Haynes Holmes had withdrawn from our fellowship. The resolution that had been passed was called the Pinkham Resolution; but the real symbol that [AUA president] Dr. Eliot's remarks brought freshly to the minds of those present at that session was Henry Pinkham himself, his hair white, his hands shaking, his voice hoarse but arresting because of its obvious sincerity, pleading with his fellow Unitarians almost with his dying breath, to wipe away a stain from their record of which John Haynes Holmes and he himself had been the victims. The response to Frederick Eliot's brief speech was immediate. The young minister who had made the motion spoke up at once. "Of course," he said; "I remember; I should have thought of that. I withdraw the motion." Because these men, together with many of the delegates present, shared common memories, the question was disposed of in less than five minutes without a dissenting voice being raised. . . . By using the symbols of communication that were peculiar to that group, and drawn from its collective memory, Dr. Eliot not only accomplished his purpose, but did it with efficiency and dispatch, protecting at the same time the social cohesion of the group.

Second, there is need for ethical discourse that transcends merely sociological, economic, or political discussions. What is justice in a particular situation? We need to look at social injustice in the light of some ultimate standard of judgment. But discourse does not stop here. It needs to be brought closer to reality by the discussion and formulation of mediating principles that are a bridge between abstract universals and specific questions of strategy and tactics. Such concepts as condemnation of poverty as a violation of freedom, putting limits on military operations, the structuring of the economy that all may share its benefits, and the maintenance of pluralism in social order are illustrative. These serve the function of narrowing the morally defensible alternatives.

Then the community of moral discourse goes on to consider these ultimate values and mediating principles in the context of specific situations, drawing on technically competent persons. The church cannot speak with special authority on matters of public policy, but it can help improve the quality of the discussion so that moral considerations will be at least one of the factors discussed. Too often overlooked in this educational role is the total church program of religious education, from cradle to grave. Every church educational curriculum should have abundant materials and resources for acquainting people with their moral tradition, ethical principles, the process of moral decision making, and how we can act in the wider world.

2. The Church as Staging Platform and Launching Pad

This model would have the church prepare and train people for social action. It encourages disciplined involvement in voluntary associations in the community or in religious social action structures at every level. This model requires the congregation to self-consciously prepare its members for responsible involvement in the community: in voluntary associations as well as in government, business, labor, nonprofits, and other sectors. In 1915 the American Unitarian Association created a Social Service Institute in Chicago to train a core of "intelligent, determined, ethically minded men and women in the churches who will have their hearts set upon the righteousness and justice in every relation of our social life."

The current emphasis of the denomination's Faith in Action Department is on training activists at the district and congregational level. An elaborate workshop has been prepared to assist congregations in the philosophy and techniques of social action. There are vast untapped resources of people, facilities, and finance represented by our districts and the network of local churches. But it is primarily the local congregation that is a potential launching pad for renewal. Is it too much to ask of our members that each of them participate in at least one community organization working for peace and justice? Clearly, we cannot make this a condition for membership, but surely we can stress the idea that to be a Unitarian Universalist is to be active in repairing the world.

The church then might conceive of itself as a place for the preparation of people for social action and as a launching platform from which to direct them to groups within the congregation or already existing voluntary associations. In this model the church would nourish voluntary associations that seek to embody something of the church's moral vision.

3. The Church as Interfaith Innovator and/or Participant

When it is discovered in the process of community research that there are social problems not effectively confronted by existing social action groups, the church can adopt the role of the social pioneer–interfaith innovator. Here, church people do spadework in new and possibly controversial areas. They begin to mobilize community resources.

They spin off a group when community support from other churches and groups has been garnered and/or participate with other groups. The approach here is coalition building. A church group begins to organize around an issue and gathers community support. Once that support has been secured, the program is adopted by a broadly based community group. The Unitarian Universalist church would seem to have a unique opportunity here, for among religious groups our openness should make us least inhibited in exploring new areas, especially controversial ones. A prime historical example is the pioneering work done by the Unitarian Laymen's League in creating a national network of memorial societies. Now this grouping is an important part of the social landscape and a leading force in consumer-based associations. Unitarian Universalist churches, their members, and ministers have been instrumental in the death with dignity (compassion in dying) movement as well, an issue many more conventional groups seek to avoid as too controversial. On issues of women in ministry and welcoming bisexual, gay, lesbian, and transgender people into our congregations, we are a beacon light for other religious movements.

The Unitarian Universalist church can also be a participant in interfaith projects. Since social issues are those on which cooperation is greatest among a community's religious institutions, and since a cooperative effort seems to be the most economical of time and resources, probably most social action should be interfaith. An example of this is the Judicial Process Commission of the Genesee Ecumenical Ministries in Rochester, New York. Here is a broadly based church–citizen group that has grown to be an important community actor in the field of criminal justice. Formed in 1972, it has become an important local model for citizen action in criminal justice. Interfaith Advocates in Rochester is a coalition of gay-friendly religious groups from virtually every faith community. Our progressive stand helps form a measuring rod for groups struggling for existence in their denominational bodies.

4. The Church as Specialized Ministry

The local church cannot be all things to all people; with limitations of staff and other resources, it cannot possibly minister to more than a very few needs of the community. However, the local congregation can form coalitions with other like-minded congregations and groups to sponsor specialized ministries. Writing about "The Crisis of the Congregation" in *Voluntary Associations: A Study of Groups in Free*

Societies, ethicist Gabriel Fackre suggests some "parables . . . [and proposals for redirection rising from them]." He believes the "heritage and resources of the church [should] be grafted onto those places and people in the world which show evidence of power and promise, on the one hand, or anguish and need, on the other. The growth of 'chaplaincies,' 'missions,' 'little congregations,' and 'vocational groups' in business, shopping centers, education, government, and the leisure and entertainment world are clues."

Examples are abundant both outside and inside Unitarian Universalism. In Dayton, Ohio, Presbyterian and United Church of Christ groupings created the Congregation of Reconciliation, which was mission-oriented in the sense that the community was its field of service. Part of its incorporation provided for a no-building program so it could concentrate its resources on social change. It functioned as a congregation with worship services and small group meetings, but its primary thrust was community action of a systemic kind. Its challenge of the local community chest, its launching of the nationwide Gulf boycott, and other projects were highly controversial and yet strikingly effective for a small group. This use of the economic boycott has been an effective model for religious groups to have a wide impact on corporate America.

Within the Unitarian Universalist movement, illustrations of this specialized ministry, some of which have already been discussed, are the Unitarian Universalist Urban Ministry, the United Nations Office in New York, the Chicago Children's Choir on Chicago's South Side, and more recently The Seventh Principle Project (eco-justice in orientation), Unitarian Universalists Acting to Stop Violence against Women, Unitarian Universalists for the Ethical Treatment of Animals, Unitarian Universalists for a Just Economic Community, Unitarian Universalists against the Death Penalty, and Interweave, a ministry advocating bisexual, gay, lesbian, and transgender rights, among others.

5. The Church as Creative Minority

It has been said that Unitarian Universalists are the bureaucrats and technicians of the establishment. From the beginning of the movement in America, this relatively small religious body has furnished leaders in virtually every field. In his monograph *Our Liberal Heritage,* Alfred S. Cole wrote, "It has been the genius of liberal churches, no matter how unresponsive they might be to new truth, how inert and dull, to nourish in their bosoms the radicals and nonconformists who eventually lifted the whole movement to new levels."

What liberal religion has lacked in numbers it has made up for in the strategic placements of its people in key positions in the society. These radicals not only lifted the movement, they lifted the nation to new levels. Particularly during the middle half of the nineteenth century, William Ellery Channing, Theodore Parker, Horace Mann, Clara Barton, Dorothea Dix, and Susan B. Anthony, among others, contributed significantly to social change. The impact of these Unitarians and Universalists was out of all proportion to the number of those who claimed that religious allegiance.

Arnold Toynbee theorized that historical change is not made by masses of people, but by a "creative minority" who are at the cutting edge of change and who are able to bring the masses with them. If so, this provides a golden opportunity for the liberal church insofar as some of the influential actors in our society are numbered among its members. Influencing the influential could be a significant contribution to social change. Church organizer Robert Bonthius writes of the "two-percent solution," by which he means the capacity for a small number of committed people to effect large social change. "Perhaps two percent of the people in a community can make some change if they are clever, know the scene and *stick with it*."

James Gustafson writes of the voluntary church that is homogeneous in its makeup. He speaks of the "possibility [that] exists in the middle and upper-middle class congregations. This is an access to influence upon persons in positions of social power. . . . The church can help the person in a position of power to interpret and understand his job, and his exercise of responsibility, as a place for moral action in the society."

The church can play a number of roles in influencing the influential. One, of course, is to include them in the community of moral discourse, thus aiding them in responsible decision making. Another is to help sustain them religiously. Influential people are often under continual pressure from all manner of publics, and their church might well become an important support for their personal needs. Finally, the denomination and the churches have hardly explored the human riches available to them in these influential persons. They could be gathered along vocational or other lines to consider social policy questions of great moment. For example, why not convene a group of doctors to consider the ethics of organ transplants, physician aid-in-dying, the problem of diminishing numbers of doctors who perform abortions, or the pressures on the medical profession with the advent of health maintenance organizations? Ministers and theologians would join in these important moral discussions. Published papers, reports, and possible action projects should emerge from such gatherings.

6. The Liberal Church as Pathfinder

Related closely to model 5, this model would have members of the liberal church be moral and philosophical troubleshooters. Leaders would address the church and its members to the cutting edge issues (e.g., bioethics, genetic engineering, limits of growth, eco-justice). This model relates directly to the liberal church as a creative minority. The Reverend Kenneth Patton challenged the Unitarian Universalist movement with these words from *The Liberal Context:*

> This is where the liberal must work, to explore the nature of these new problems, and to seek out and experiment with possible solutions to them. We should be the moral and philosophical trouble-shooters of the human race, and the poets and artists of the new world. If we do not accept this task as our own, we do not deserve to call ourselves by the noble word liberal.

He goes on to point out that a general moral consensus has been forged on many issues (e.g., civil rights for African Americans are no longer morally in dispute, although implementation of these rights is far from complete). Patton feels that the liberal church should spend its energies at the frontiers of morality, in genetic engineering, cybernetics, and other issues where the moral consensus has yet to be formed.

A prime example of this approach is the Religious Society of Friends, which has published several influential documents created by *ad hoc* study groups of experts, producing such works as *Who Shall Live? Man's Control over Birth and Death,* an exploration of the meaning of life, birth, and death in the biological sciences; *Search for Peace in the Middle East,* a controversial declaration about that volatile situation; and *Towards a Quaker View of Sex,* another controversial statement, all extremely influential documents produced at relatively low cost by a relatively small group. Certainly, our pioneering work in sexuality education (along with the United Church of Christ) with the *Our Whole Lives* program can be counted in this category. There is no reason why the liberal church cannot create other documents as important for social change as these.

7. Ecclesiola in Ecclesia

The principle here is to create a small, disciplined group of activists who would covenant together in spiritual disciplines and involvement in voluntary associations. They would meet regularly for worship and ethical reflection on their community involvements. This model is that of a small, committed group of church people working both inside and outside the church to effect social change. This is a primary group with person-to-person relations among folk who have taken on themselves the disciplines of social responsibility.

Significant social change often does not come through consensus of large groups, but through the disciplined labor of a small group to influence larger constituencies. We cannot expect a whole religious movement to be at the cutting edge of critical social issues. Leadership is forging a consensus, not waiting for it to happen. The activists sit in the pews with people who are often skeptical of what the activists do. Initially, we can only hope for mutual respect, address to the issue, and eventual change. I think of the Task Force on Economic Justice appointed by UUA President Paul Carnes in the late seventies. As chair of that Task Force, I know firsthand the fear, the skepticism, and even the hostility with which we were greeted in some quarters. Early on we gave up writing a consensus statement for the denomination on economic justice. However, the dialogues launched in those days I believe helped pave the way for creation of Unitarian Universalists for a Just Economic Community and eventual passage of economic justice resolutions in the late nineties.

James Hunt develops James Luther Adams's "ecclesiola in ecclesia" (the little church within the larger church) concept as follows in *Voluntary Associations: A Study of Groups in Free Societies:*

> [T]here the vitalities of the sect become manifest: intimate fellowship, explicit faith, the expression of concerns, the identification of adversaries, the achievement of consensus, the protection of the freedom of the spirit, the definition of models, the practice of self-criticism of the group, and the disciplined definition and application of norms to the whole life of the believers.

Adams himself was a charter member of a group called Brothers of the Way. The group covenanted together, and every member was required to adopt some spiritual discipline, to meet together for discussion of religious and social questions, and to participate in the program of one controversial secular organization working for human good in the community. One could, for example, be a member of a library board of trustees only if that group were besieged with calls for censorship. This kind of intentional group is built on the kind of internal discipline so essential for effective social action. Here is one basis for a constituency of conscience, a highly disciplined and trained group that can be leaven for the loaf, whether the loaf be church or society.

8. The Church as Corporate Actor

Finally, the church should function in the community as an institution. The corporate role of the church is inevitable and should be made conscious. Any voluntary association has a character in the community. It is compelled to say yes or no to requests for space, funds, and/or group support. Ways of taking a stand can be carefully thought out to preserve democratic traditions and individual liberties.

Here we come to the most complex and controversial mode of relating the local congregation to the society. The typical question raised, with usually an implied negative answer, is, "Should the local congregation take a stand?" This issue has been raised at denominational, district, and congregational levels by many, including the Unitarian Universalists for Freedom of Conscience. At this point, several things ought to be said in addressing this question.

First, it is inevitable that the local congregation will have a corporate role. No matter how much members of a church may wish to have their church stay out of politics or social issues, no matter how much they may wish to stress personal witness and ignore public witness, it is impossible. The very existence of the church as a social institution constitutes a corporate witness. Theologian and educator Angus H. MacLean writes of the "problem of corporate goodness" in *The Wind in Both Ears:*

> The fact is that a corporation such as a church has character, inescapably so. It cannot be neutral. Despite the weight of feeling on this matter among us, if the church cannot operate as our agent of good, cannot be committed in any way, how can we expect our nation to have moral concerns and act ethically? How can it have moral significance and character? A sense of certainty deserts me, but it doesn't at this point. The church can not be less significant ethically as a corporate unit than its individual members are supposed to be.

If a church decides to move from center city to suburb, this says something about its corporate witness. Churches are constantly confronted with community groups, often controversial ones, asking for meeting space, contributions, endorsement, and other forms of support. The churches must respond yes or no, and in so doing they are acting corporately. The only question is whether this corporate witness will be an explicit outgrowth of a community of moral discourse in which there has been broad participation or will it be action by default based on low participation, inadequate information, inarticulate rationale, and/or emotional outbursts.

For example, during the Vietnam War I withheld my telephone excise tax as an antiwar protest. When my wages were finally about to be garnished, I decided to pay my bill with a check written on a peace poster, "War is not healthy for children and other living things." Members of the congregation joined me in a moving street liturgy outside the federal building where I paid my modest bill. When members of the church called a congregational meeting by petition, according to the bylaws, urging the church to withhold its telephone tax, the resolution was defeated—I being in the minority. One member of the congregation, a lawyer, resigned in protest—not because of the vote, for he opposed the action proposed, but because we had called a meeting to take a position on the issue. I wrote him asking how he as a lawyer could deny the legal remedy provided in the church bylaws for a church meeting by petition of requisite members? There was no way to avoid taking a stand. He made no response.

James Gustafson points out that the community of moral discourse must also be a community of action. Gustafson asks, "Do the churches have such institutional power and authority? On the whole, the answer is no. Should the churches have such power and authority? My answer is that they need more than they have and that they will need more in the next third of the century than they have needed in the past."

As William Gardiner of the UUA Faith in Action Department puts it succinctly: "the idea that the church should take no position on moral issues seems to be self-contradictory—for taking no action is in itself a form [of] action. . . . Not to decide is to decide."

There are a variety of modes of corporate social action. The use of the building for community groups, church-sponsored forums, and programs (social justice centers, alternative schools) is one example. The permanent housing of social action groups is an important contribution to social change since these groups most often operate on a minimal budget and are dependent on gifts in kind.

Second, the church is an institution with financial resources that might be used to make an impact on social change. The religious communities of America control billions of dollars of real estate and securities. Furthermore, billions more are contributed each year by the members. Religious communities have become leaders in stockholder resolution actions, dropping the moral plumbline over corporate policy. Seldom, if ever, do such actions win in the sense of passing such resolutions, but they do serve to publicly embarrass corporations into improved social behavior. By and large, religious groups have used their stock as leverage for corporate policy rather than seeking purity for the church portfolio by means of divestment.

While the Unitarian Universalist movement has modest resources, those we have give significant potential for investing in justice. According to the 1999–2000 *Directory* of the Association, over $143 million went into the budgets of member societies. The UUA itself has assets of over $100 million. The pension plan for church employees has provision for social equity funds among the many investment choices. The Unitarian Universalist Association has developed a document on the social responsibility of the churches in investments and has instituted an ethical audit of its own portfolio. It has participated in various interfaith programs as well. Many local congregations have followed suit, listing social responsibility as one investment criterion, along with the customary investment standards of growth and security.

Finally, there are countless other ways in which the local church *qua* church can assume social responsibility: sponsorship of housing projects for low-income and elderly people, providing of community centers, and much more. Increasingly, our congregations are involved in hands-on projects: homeless shelters, soup kitchens, school tutoring. This is a welcome change from the justice-by-committee resolution approach, but it is important not only to provide generally prosperous people with direct contact with the poor and oppressed, but also to give firsthand experience that can be translated into more caring and knowing social action. More recently, several of our congregations have been involved, usually with other congregations, in community organizing. For example, the Reverend Suzanne R. Spencer describes her experience with the Industrial Areas Foundation in VOICE, Valley Organized in Community Efforts, part of a network of the IAF founded by Saul Alinsky in 1940. The UUA Grants Panel helped fund an interfaith community organizing effort in New Orleans in which Unitarian Universalist congregations played a significant role. Interfaith Impact of New York State is an effort by

Unitarian Universalists, mainline Protestants, and Reform Jews to advocate for progressive policies at the state level, as more and more social service programs devolve there.

The question most often raised, however, is still, "Should the church speak out?" There is an almost fetish-like quality to the urgency with which some would have the church make pronouncements on all manner of public issues. For some it becomes an end in itself, rather than a means by which mobilization for change is initiated. Resolutions without a concrete program of implementation are social witness, not social action—sometimes useful, seldom decisive. David O. Moberg has made the following critique of such statements in his study, *The Church as a Social Institution:*

> The gap between the quality of many Protestant social pronouncements and their support by members is due to at least six major barriers to social effectiveness: (1) The right to believe and worship according to one's own conviction. This freedom for something is often construed as freedom from the claims of the gospel. Separatism with regard to social issues results. (2) American individualism has carried over into a personal emphasis on presenting the gospel and often has prevented social teachings from taking root. (3) The idea of community, a sense of fellowship and oneness in the church, has only recently begun to develop as a theological concept. (4) Because of the dominance of business economics, and technology, any criticism of the underlying philosophy of American business seems to bite the hands that feed every one. Many social issues are therefore considered to be matters of business or technical skill rather than of morals. (5) Clergymen often unwittingly endorse the status quo because they lack a solid grounding in the social sciences and in some of the more demanding disciplines of religion. (6) The tremendous complexity of American society has eroded the sense of competence to remedy its ills. Instead of confidence that all evils will give way before the sheer determination that righteousness should prevail, there is now a tendency to leave things to the "experts" or to let them work themselves out.

The controversy surrounding resolutions at denominational, district, and local levels sometimes seems too great a price to pay. Some ministers and laypeople speak of the noncreedal nature of the liberal church and object to anything that smacks of a social creed. Still others cite the tyranny of the majority in making decisions. These arguments, however, can be countered by indicating that the church's indifference on public issues constitutes a creed of silence. At least as fearful as the tyranny of the majority is the tyranny of the minority.

After considering many pros and cons, the 1967 Commission on the Free Church in a Changing World, in its section "Ethics and Social Action," concluded: "The Commission recommends that local churches devise methods of taking stands on social issues with due regard for democratic processes and the meaning of the experience for those participating." The UUA Commission on Appraisal's 1997 report, *Interdependence,* has an illuminating discussion of this issue and guidelines for action. It concluded, "[We] believe it is better to err on the side of action rather than inaction."

There are guidelines for enabling the church to act corporately. In a number of instances a church's taking a stand is important in forming a moral consensus. Such stand taking must be seen both in the sense of speaking to the society and of speaking to the church as part of a continuing dialogue. Some guidelines follow: (1) The importance of resolutions by the local congregation is in direct proportion to the degree of participation by the whole congregation. (2) The importance of taking a stand is in proportion to the proximity of the issue to the local congregation. The closer the issue, the more important for discussion and action. (3) The importance of resolutions is in proportion to the quality of the plan for follow-up action. Discussions in the community of moral discourse ought to have built into them an action component, else the seriousness of the resolution can be challenged. Otherwise, resolutions will be, as one skeptic has said, like "petitionary prayer."

There are alternatives to the often divisive question of taking an official congregational stand. One is to launch letter-writing, fax, telegram, and e-mail campaigns on issues during after-church social hours. Some churches have created a Committee of Correspondence, named after the Revolutionary War groups that rallied support for independence. This approach consists of a letter-writing table with information on the issue, maps of political jurisdictions so that writers will be sure who their representatives are, sample letters, paper, envelopes, and stamps. The issue is introduced from the pulpit for action. Another possibility is to develop a letter to the editor or public official signed by members of the congregation *qua* members, indicating the sense of those signing it. A social responsibility committee often can take a stand as a committee, not implicating the whole church.

In a Chicago Unitarian church the following procedure was established: A task force group formed around a specific concern. Membership in the task force was contingent on belonging to one voluntary association focusing on the issue. This group would periodically report to the minister, who would then preach a sermon on the issue. Following this, a town meeting of the whole congregation was called to discuss the issue in depth. Then a resolution was considered and acted on, as the sense of that meeting, not an official statement of the church. Plans for implementation were included. This procedure incorporates some of the guidelines already listed. While there is no substitute for the serious dialogue of the whole congregation on a matter of substance, these alternatives may be utilized either as a substitute for such action or as a steppingstone to that action.

In one dramatic illustration of a congregation taking a significant stand, the First Unitarian Church of Portland, Oregon, stood corporately against an initiative that would deny legislation on behalf of gay rights. This "ribbon project" was launched by the minister, the Reverend Marilyn Sewell, and then supported by the congregation. They delineated a "hate-free zone" around property that the church owned in the city of Portland and wrapped a large ribbon around the space, while actively engaging in lobbying for defeat of the legislation.

All Souls Church (Unitarian Universalist) in New York City created a Children's Task Force to address conditions in New York's Prince George Welfare Hotel where 1,100 homeless children "were warehoused with their families." As Senior Minister Forrest Church points out, "There is no conflict between church and school. In the liberal tradition, our object is not to save souls but to serve them."

In May 1983, Memorial Unitarian Universalist Society in Syracuse, New York, voted to provide sanctuary for El Salvadoran refugees fleeing their country because they were targets of the infamous death squads of the Salvadoran military. It was a controversial issue, but it was done in conjunction with other religious communities. After the peace accords, members of the coalition accompanied refugees back to their communities, and material aid was sent to Syracuse's sister community of La Estancia. This led to concern for the School of the Americas (SOA), a U.S. training center for Latin American military personnel who were often implicated in human rights abuses. Members of the church became active in protest against funding of what was called the School of the Assassins. Five members of the congregation, including the Reverend Nicholas Cardell, minister emeritus of the society, spent six months in jail after being arrested during a protest action at Fort Benning, Georgia, site of the SOA. At the 1998

UUA General Assembly in Rochester, New York, the congregation submitted a successful Resolution of Immediate Witness urging Congress to close the school.

These eight models for social action are designed to stimulate dialogue on the ways in which the church might organize to act on its society. It is crucial that such dialogue be a vital part of the total program of the congregation, with heavy congregational involvement. This corporate element is essential if effective action is to emerge. The church should see itself as an agency for social change, not simply a place where individual social involvement is tolerated or merely encouraged. If social action in the church is left to a marginal few, the social strength of the church is greatly diminished. The greater the involvement of the total congregation in planning and implementing various modes of social action, the greater its impact will be. Unitarian Universalists must not be frozen out of prophetic social action.

CHAPTER EIGHT

Ten Commandments
for Social Action

I have tried to demonstrate that the liberal church (Unitarian Universalist) lives under a prophetic imperative, a religious mandate for the corporate address of the church to the systemic problems of the communities in which it lives. In discussing this mandate we have seen that a new social gospel will be informed by both the mistakes and insights of the historic social gospel movement. It will be more firmly grounded in a religious base, will have a more sober assessment of the finitude of human nature, will more fully recognize the stubbornness of the demonic in history, and will sense the need for a much more disciplined approach to social change.

I have indicated something of the obstacles in the path of creating a new social gospel. Chief among these is the demonic of privatization, a turning inward from social problems. The increasing pace of contemporary life with increasing demands from the marketplace exacerbates the problem. Add to that the tremendous complexity of the social process and the corresponding sense of helplessness on the part of individuals, and the stumbling blocks become awesome. These factors, among others, suggest the need for a highly motivated and disciplined cadre of people who will with patience and determination spend a lifetime in what Eric Lindeman calls the "humdrum work of democracy." Furthermore, I have contended that liberal religion has the capacity to inspire such commitment and that the liberal church is the spiritual center in which people can mobilize themselves for such efforts.

I have argued that the resources for this new social gospel are available in the history, theology, ethics, and sociology of this religious community. The history of the Unitarian Universalist movement reveals a continual emphasis on religion as a social principle. We have seen the trend from social service in the early nineteenth century to the systemic change approach of the fourth quarter of the twentieth century. From William Ellery Channing's first timid prophetic voice to the serious and focused work of the Unitarian Universalist Service Committee, we have seen the prophetic imperative in action.

Henry Nelson Wieman's formulation of creativity provides a humanist frame of reference for social action. This creativity consists of the natural forces of the cosmos that have not only created humanity, but also provide the focus for humanity increasingly to direct that creativity toward the Beloved Community. While the horizontal transcendence of religious humanism is only one theological approach to social action, it is one that needs clear statement, which has been lacking. My own conceptualization is intended to be a contribution in this regard. The decisive point for the prophetic imperative is that social action must be grounded in and emerge from a carefully thought out and well-articulated theology.

Reverence for life, I believe, provides the ethical basis for social action. This motif can appeal broadly to the Unitarian Universalist community as it mandates individuals and communities to serve life by expanding its quality. This ethical base is informed by the insight that ethics really constitutes unenforceable obligations, that love is the expression of reverence for life in personal relations, justice in social relations, and trusteeship in our relations with the nonhuman natural world. The creation of the Beloved Community of Love and Justice was suggested as the covenantal basis for liberal religion.

The church, among other things, is a social institution and has both real and potential power in the social order. It is one among many voluntary associations that contribute both vision and energy in seeking the common good. It differs from many self-interest groups in that its chief end is more the public good than the self-serving of a particular community. I have developed eight models by which a local congregation might organize itself for social action. Ministers and laity have a common responsibility to create a community of moral discourse and action. This dimension of congregational life should not be seen as an addendum to the more traditional features of worship, caring ministry, and religious education, but as one essential role without which the church is less than the church. Social action, then, becomes not a hobby or avocation of a small coterie, but the overflowing concern of the church for the world of which it is a part. It becomes one vital expression of the very nature of the church as a Beloved Community in miniature.

The intimate relationship between religious education and social justice reminds us of our responsibility to pass on the torch of justice to those who follow. This is a too often neglected aspect of social responsibility programs, the need to replenish the justice workers. A case study of one way of working out the prophetic imperative has been presented, not as a model for replication but as stimulus for congregations to do their own institutional soul searching and find their own *modus operandi.* Without institutional embodiment the prophetic imperative is simply engaging in self-indulgent rhetoric.

The liberal church is neither a great Christian joke nor a subordinate amusement, and it should never become merely a political satrap. There is always danger that this will be the case, however. The historical pendulum seems to swing between periods of great social involvement and of intense introspection. It is my hope that the time is at hand for a renewal of the social gospel. I write in the faith that religiously committed men and women can seize the time to quicken and deepen the age-old quest for social justice.

From my time as an activist I have, I think, learned some things about social action. I share them in the form of Ten Commandments. As you read them I ask you to keep in mind the words of a Turkish proverb: "If you would speak the truth, keep one foot in the stirrup of the saddle."

1. Thou shalt always seek to make tangible in actions what is intangible in values. To be biblical, "Faith without works is dead" (James 2:17).

2. Thou shalt consider thyself a fulcrum to change the world. The Greek Archimedes once said, "Give me where to stand, and I will move the earth." Thou art a lever to move things to a better place; each action has cosmic consequences.

3. Thou shalt carry a newspaper in one hand and a Bible (or its equivalent for you) in the other. Social action grows out of a value system, be it religious or secular, be it the Koran or the Constitution, be it the Hebrew prophets or Ralph Nader.

4. Thou shalt remember that many are called, but most are frozen. Beware being like Voltaire's Candide, who, seeing the evils of the world, decided he would simply cultivate his garden. I have nothing against gardens, only against those who spend all their free time there.

5. Thou shalt resist burnout; thou shalt invest thyself for the long haul, yea even beyond the next issue. One of my friends hath said the world is changed by those who stay at meetings until the very end. Thou shalt remember that to love justice is not an occasional pursuit, but a way of living. Be thou not summer citizens who quit

their work when icy drafts of apathy and reaction cool their ardor. Thy goals will not be achieved during thy lifetime.

6. Thou shalt do thy homework. Blessed (and effective) are the informed. Ye shall know the facts, and the facts shall make thee powerful. And remember George Bernard Shaw's dictum: The world's best reformers are those who begin on themselves.

7. Thou shalt think globally and act locally. Thou shalt see thy work in its larger context of meaning and action and do thy own small part well. Think of the cartoon of Don Quixote and Sancho Panza approaching a great modern city of skyscrapers. Saith Sancho to Don Quixote, "Tell me again how we're going to fight city hall." By thinking globally and acting locally.

8. Thou shalt change the world (fight city hall) one step at a time. As it hath been said by Lao Tze, "The journey of a thousand miles begins with a single step." Thou shalt have thy great goals before thee, but thou shalt also have thy objectives (specific, measurable, achievable, and consonant with thy values), thy strategies, thy tactics, and thy timelines—especially thy timelines. Thou shalt adhere unto them.

9. Thou shalt constitute thy group as a community of moral discourse and action. Thou canst not change the world by thyself. Harken unto thy comrades and they will harken unto thee. Act faithfully and thy comrades will do likewise (hope we always).

10. Thou shalt be a happy warrior. Grouches seldom change the world. Prepare thyself for a "joyous struggle" (Fred Shuttlesworth as he lay bleeding from a beating in a civil rights demonstration). Keep thy sense of humor, for thou wilt need it in a crazy world. Celebrate life in all thy going out and coming in, yea, from this day forth.

Ultimately, I am chastened and sobered by these hard words spoken by a soldier of the Republican Army in the Spanish Civil War: "People who have principles but no programs, turn out in the end to have no principles."

CHAPTER NINE

To Change the World

The First Unitarian Church of Rochester has a long history of engagement with the world in an effort to transform it. The first Women's Rights Convention in 1848 was adjourned from Seneca Falls to the First Unitarian Church in Rochester. The Boy's Evening Home was established around the turn of the century, a pioneering settlement house project. Susan B. Anthony, who worshipped here for many years, needs no detailing. The Visiting Nurse Service was initiated by members of the church. The Mother's Consultation Center, forerunner of Planned Parenthood, was founded in the church's parish house. The Rochester Memorial Society was founded by church members. In the sixties the congregation voted to support Saul Alinsky's FIGHT organization, a black empowerment group, and to declare symbolic sanctuary for draft resisters in 1969.

But by 1978 social responsibility had slackened here, as elsewhere, and a change was needed. The church's social action effort seemed scattered, consisting of the work of the ministers or the Social Responsibility Committee (SRC) or just a few committed individuals. In the fall of that year a new program was launched, and it has guided our efforts since. This overview is intended to tell that story and to suggest that other groups might consider a similar approach. Over the years the program has grown and evolved; changes in the processes may be instituted to keep up with the increasing number of components, but the basic program stays the same.

This chapter is the contribution of Richard S. Gilbert, Nancy Eckerson Fitts, and Alison Wilder, First Unitarian Church, 220 Winton Road South, Rochester, NY 14610.

RATIONALE

The program is based on a particular understanding of the nature of the liberal church as outlined in Chapter Six. There are four dimensions of religious life in the church: (1) the church as worshipping community out of a spiritual core, (2) the church as caring community in which a mutual ministry operates to meet personal needs, (3) the church as a community of life-span religious education, and (4) the church as a community of moral discourse and social action.

The key is that each of these segments touches every other segment. They are understood not as administrative categories, but as functions of the church occurring at many programmatic places. These aspects of the total program are interdependent. No one succeeds unless all the others succeed. But the core of the total process is worship, indicating the religious underpinning of the whole. In the moral discourse and social action segment we engage in an ongoing conversation about moral values in the Unitarian Universalist tradition. What remains is translating this moral discourse into social action.

The key concepts are involvement and accountability. We have had as many as 125 people involved, in contrast to times when maintaining a single social responsibility committee was a struggle. They are involved because there are specific tasks to be done and because they know that the congregation supports their efforts. The social responsibility program is not a special interest group, but an integral part of congregational life. The whole congregation is accountable, just as it is for worship, education, and mutual ministry.

SOCIAL RESPONSIBILITY COUNCIL

Most of the social action of our church is carried out by task forces that address issues chosen annually at a congregational meeting. Their activities are coordinated by the Social Responsibility Council (SRC), a steering committee. The SRC is composed mainly of representatives of task forces and other groups that are gathered administratively under the SRC umbrella. These other groups include ad hoc committees and Unitarian Universalist affiliates like the Unitarian Universalist Service Committee (UUSC) and the Unitarian Universalist United Nations Office (UUUNO). Also attending SRC monthly meetings are the ministers, when time permits, a group leader who represents the SRC to the church council, the SRC chair or cochairs, the SRC secretary, and other individuals who care about the church's social action but have no official capacity. At the monthly meetings, members report on their group's activities, set policy, plan all-SRC events and fundraisers, and allocate committee funds. This committee has the following functions:

1. Facilitate the selection of task forces.

2. Monitor existing task forces and ad hoc committees, assist them in keeping the congregation informed of their activities, channel comments from the congregation and relevant mail to them, and assist task force leaders (often relatively new church members) in becoming familiar with how to get things done at church.

3. Act as financial agent for the church's social responsibility funds, both those funds raised by task forces or ad hoc committees and those allocated in the church budget to the SRC. SRC divides its budget among task forces, ad hoc committees, denominational groups like UUSC, and other community and charitable groups.

4. Manage two grants programs. A small fund, created in 1984 from the church budget and augmented by contributions and fundraising activities, has grown large enough to warrant a grants panel, which now annually awards modest sums to local groups devoted to community improvement (see Samples 1–3 for more information about the application and selection processes and a copy of the application). A second grants program, funded by a donation, funds activities that promote peace through international understanding. The SRC Council also administers building-use credits by which community groups with similar interests can use church facilities at reduced rates.

5. Act as liaison with denominational structures like the Unitarian Universalist Association (UUA), the St. Lawrence Unitarian Universalist District (SLUUD), UUSC, and UUUNO in regard to social action issues. Our church calendar includes an annual Social Responsibility Sunday in the fall, usually in conjunction with the congregational meeting to select task forces, two UUSC Sundays, a UN Sunday, an Urban Ministry Sunday, and an Earth Day Sunday.

6. Handle SRC mail, serve as liaison with community organizations, and keep the congregation informed on general social action topics not covered by a specific task force or ad hoc committee or group, such as UU General Assembly resolutions.

7. Report periodically to the board of trustees and to the congregation through meetings and the church newsletter.

8. Sponsor a weekly Committee of Correspondence Table focused on an issue chosen by SRC and brought to the attention of the congregation during the announcements in the Sunday services (see proposal memo in Sample 4).

SELECTION OF ISSUES

During the first few years that our church's selection process was in effect, a poll was taken in the spring to find out what issues were of concern to the congregation. Then the SRC obtained advocates for each issue who would research the subject and present it for consideration at the annual fall congregational meeting devoted to social responsibility.

More recently, with several task forces already in place, we have let groups form and provide their own leadership at the annual meeting on social responsibility. Perhaps having the poll was a consciousness-raising activity, suggesting topics that would not otherwise be addressed. General Assembly resolutions are another source of possible issues for task forces to address. The number of task forces has stayed relatively constant at five to seven.

In any case, before the fall congregational meeting, groups wishing to be approved as official task forces must obtain signatures of five church members willing to work actively with the task force and five others who support the issue but may not have time to devote to it. The petition is submitted to the SRC, along with a description of proposed goals and activities of the group, which the SRC publicizes to the congregation by means of a flyer in the church newsletter before the meeting (see Sample 5 for a copy of the petition). Traditionally, this congregational meeting has been held on a Sunday evening. During the meeting, an advocate from each group is allowed five minutes to present the goals and proposed activities for the following year. A brief question period follows each presentation (see Sample 6 for guidelines concerning controversial issues).

After all the issues are presented, the next step depends on the number of task forces applying. If only a few groups are applying, the SRC may move to approve them all. If there are more groups than the SRC feels that the church can handle, considering the office support, meeting room space, and volunteer resources available, the congregation decides which ones to support. The actual methods of voting have varied, but they are restricted somewhat by our bylaws. Usually, some form of rank ordering is utilized to reduce the groups to the number that the congregation feels it can handle. It is helpful to have a blackboard or easel to list the issues and printed ballots for voting. During the counting of ballots, other reports are given or other business transacted.

A task force is approved for only one year. If, after consultation with the SRC, the group agrees that it wishes to continue the following year, it goes through the same petition process and voting again the next September. Groups that are not selected for task force status may either operate as *ad hoc* committees with reduced status and privileges or disband. They may try again the next year to become a task force. Task forces that have been in existence but are not reapproved deserve a public thank you for their work; they may spend any money in their account by June 30 or it reverts to the SRC account.

IMPLEMENTATION

Task Force Responsibilities

As soon as a task force is approved, it chooses temporary leaders (at the congregational meeting if possible) and a first meeting date and and then conducts business as it wishes. A task force meets once or twice a month. If appropriate it will join other groups in the community concerned with the same issue. It may enter coalitions, participate in demonstrations, and, with others, place ads in the paper. Other responsibilities are as follows:

1. Submit a budget to the SRC, giving tentative plans for using the money. The SRC chairperson(s) is to be kept informed of expenses incurred and whether funds are to be used from its fundraising account or from the church-provided SRC budget. It may raise funds by sales, serving lunches, and special projects within the guidelines specified by the Finance Committee. (After-church bagel sales are a favorite fundraiser.)

2. Send a task force representative to all SRC steering committee meetings; it is essential that the SRC be informed of all task force or ad hoc committee plans and activities to minimize the problem of multiple events scheduled in the same time block and to allow cooperation between groups. If only a few task forces are applying and there is no other business to conduct at this meeting (so we know it will be a short meeting), we sometimes hold it after church on Sunday.

3. Educate the congregation about its particular issues by means of the Sunday Morning Forum (a forty-five-minute meeting period

between church services), information tables, flyers and newsletter items, and bulletin board space; it may sponsor activities such as writing to officials or attending conferences. A task force may request the board to call a congregational meeting to take action on a task force resolution.

4. In the spring a task force gives an annual written report to the SRC, to be published in the annual church report, and discusses with the SRC its possible continuance in the fall.

Task Force Privileges

Official task force status carries benefits:

1. Funding from the SRC budget
2. Free meeting space and use of church buildings for major events
3. Priority for staff support, including preference as a sermon topic
4. Flyers in the church newsletter or announcements in Sunday programs; "air" time during the church service
5. Space on the lobby bulletin board and a church mailbox
6. When addressing an issue in the larger community, the task force can identify itself as an official task force of the First Unitarian Church, thus giving greater emphasis to its endorsement or objections. In accordance with established church policy, a task force may not claim to represent the entire congregation.

Ad Hoc Committees

These groups may still receive free room space for meetings and access to the newsletter and Sunday program. However, they are not guaranteed the support and high priority given to the official task forces. They may hold fundraising lunches and can request funding from the SRC. They must report to the SRC.

Strategic Planning Process for Use in UU Groups

The strategic planning process suggested here is a composite drawn from many other variations on this theme. It provides a disciplined program of reflection and action on social problems by a religious community. This planning process creates a framework for decision making and action (see Samples 7 and 8 for a historical example and a sample worksheet). Objectives and strategies are continually under review.

Step One: Definition of the Social Problem to Be Addressed

This is a one-sentence statement of a specific problem that indicates who or what is doing what to whom and where. It should be a problem about which there is high interest in the group, the possibility of meaningful action, and a sense of appropriateness.

Step Two: Statement of Environmental Assumptions

Environmental assumptions describe briefly the social context in which the problem is found. This would include stating why it is a problem, who suffers from it, how they are affected, and the economic, political, and social factors involved.

Step Three: Statement of Religious Assumptions

The religious assumptions are the value base out of which a group operates. These would be affirmations, theological and ethical in nature, that describe the motivation of the group in attacking a particular problem. Statements about ultimate concerns, human nature, and life meaning would be included. They should state why the problem represents injustice and why achievement of the goal is a step toward justice.

Step Four: Statement of the Action Goal

Here is a declaration of the ultimate aim of the group with respect to the social problem selected. It should be:

Specific, as to time, place, and people.

Measurable, so that the group may chart its progress or lack thereof.

Achievable, something that is reasonably within the group's capacity.

Consonant with the religious values of the group.

Step Five: Selection of a Strategy or Strategies

This involves examination of the alternative plans that might be chosen to achieve the goal. One or more strategies might be selected from many possibilities. A strategy is an overall plan by which a group guides itself, a "how" of social responsibility that states who does what.

Step Six: Development and Implementation of Tactics

Tactics are the specific actions that constitute a strategy. They indicate assignments of action to particular people, the details of what they are to do, and a time line for reporting on and completing the tasks. The development of tactics should result in an overall time line that establishes an end to the project. The time line will form the core of the agenda for future meetings.

Step Seven: Evaluation of the Project

Evaluation should be a part of every meeting, checking on all the above points to be sure the group still supports the items chosen. Evaluation should be done in the following areas: (1) What changes have been made that lead to problem solution? (2) How is the group functioning in terms of morale, efficiency, and meaning of the task? (3) What has been learned about social change and about personal growth in social responsibility?

CONCLUSION

The process, while far from perfect, has worked to involve more members of the congregation in social responsibility and has given this program greater visibility and support from the whole congregation.

Among the task forces that have been supported are the following: Accessibility (to the church for those with disabilities); Alcohol and Drugs; Central and Latin American Affairs; Community against Racism; Energy Issues; Environmental Issues; Gay, Lesbian, Bisexual, and Transgender Concerns; Hunger–Housing–Homelessness; Middle East; Iraq and the Gulf; Nuclear Arms Issues; Reproductive Choice; Rochesterians against Intoxicated Driving; Women's Equity, and the School Partnership Program (22/UU/CS), a working relationship with two inner-city public schools that was initiated in 1988.

Since the process was launched, three congregational meetings have been called to act on a recommendation of a task force: to endorse a nuclear freeze, to offer sanctuary for Central American refugees, and to declare the church a nuclear-free zone. We have not escaped controversy in this process, but have learned something of how to deal with it creatively. Social responsibility remains a vital part of our congregational life, but only in the context of a total religious community as outlined in the rationale. We continue to refine the process and welcome suggestions.

The most recent congregational project, in 1999, was raising $30,000 from the church budget, members, fundraisers, foundations, and others interested for a playground for an inner-city elementary school. The program emerged out of a Church Council retreat from the desire to have an all-congregational project that could include all ages. After a year of research, including consulting with government and community groups, a school playground on a public city park was selected. In addition to fundraising and the logistics of working with a playground vendor, there was the work of installation, which was an all-congregational and all-school effort. The program culminated with a celebration with the school, the neighborhood, and the wider community.

The 22/UU/CS School Partnership Program has been the most successful of our task forces, providing about fifty volunteers, materials collected one Sunday a month, and funds to provide field trips for an inner-city school that would otherwise have none. It has received several awards, now has a special status beyond a task force with a part-time volunteer coordinator paid from the church budget, and was described in a workshop at the 1998 General Assembly. This project is primarily social service in nature. However, there is opportunity for social witness for inner-city public education, social education as the congregation learns about the problems of urban education, and social action when the congregation is invited to advocate for increased support of public education.

Sample 1

Social Justice Outreach Grants

I. BACKGROUND

In 1983, the congregation approved a Social Investment Fund to be administered by the Social Responsibility Committee (SRC). The money has come from the church budget and from interest earned on a Social Investment Charter Fund, which receives money from gifts and fundraisers. In the early years, groups applying for funding filled out short application forms and then made presentations at the March congregational meeting. The congregation rank-ordered their choices, votes were counted, and the SRC drafted a motion to approve the top choices. By 1991 the large number of groups applying made this process cumbersome: presenters had too little time to make an adequate appeal and counting the votes took too long. So a new procedure using a small grants panel was adopted.

II. GUIDELINES FOR GROUPS AND PROPOSALS TO BE FUNDED

Groups receiving funds must be local (greater Rochester area), nonpartisan, voluntary associations, not for profit, and designed for community improvement. Projects to be funded may be for social service, social education, social witness, or social action. Proposals must be specific, measurable, achievable, and congruent with UU values. Groups directly supported by a task force are not eligible for social justice outreach grants; a group may not receive social justice outreach grants more than two years in a row.

III. OPERATION OF SOCIAL JUSTICE OUTREACH GRANTS

1. Applications are available in the church office. The person taking an application must sign a sheet in the application folder, giving name, phone number, and program to be sponsored, so that the SRC will know whom to contact about the date and time to make a presentation to the Grants Panel.
2. Applications are submitted by a church-member sponsor who is familiar with the program being proposed. The sponsor should visit the site of the program and talk to a director or other administrator about the need, other financing available, supervision of expenditure of funding, and evaluation of it afterward.
3. The signatures of ten church members who support the program must appear on the application, along with the name of the sponsor.
4. Applications are due on a designated date in January or February.

continues

Sample 1 *(continued)*

5. A Social Justice Outreach Grants Panel, to oversee the operation of the grants, is appointed by the SRC. The panel consists of seven church members, with staggered terms of three years each; some, but not all of the members should be from the SRC. Members are approved by the board and then by the congregation at the fall congregational meeting. The chair of the SRC will attend panel meetings, but vote only in case of a tie. Panel members may not sponsor a group applying for Social Investment funds; a panel member with a strong interest in a group applying for Social Investment money may not vote on that proposal.

Selection Process

1. Each year the panel sets dates in January or February, when all applicants will have fifteen-minute appointments to make presentations.
2. Panel members read the applications before the day of the presentations and have questions ready.
3. The congregation is invited to listen to presentations and ask questions of presenters if there is time after panel questioning. However, members of the audience may only question presenters, not debate among themselves. Members of the audience may make statements of one to two minutes in support of a candidate group if the panel agrees that sufficient time is available. Lengthy presentations are not permitted.
4. After all presentations have been made, the panel meets in private to choose the groups to be funded.
5. Criteria used to choose may include need, other sources of funding, contribution to the community, number of persons that will benefit, and thoroughness of plan.
6. Applicants will be notified of the panel's decisions by mail after they are approved by the congregation.

Announcement to the Congregation

1. The board is notified of the panel's choices.
2. The panel places a notice of its choices with a short description of each group in a newsletter two weeks before the March congregational meeting.
3. The panel presents the chosen groups in the form of a motion for approval by the congregation.

Evaluation

1. All groups receiving funding must return a written evaluation form (included with the check for their grant) to the Social Investment Fund Panel telling how the money was spent. The evaluations are due by December 1 of the funding year.

continues

Sample 1 *(continued)*

2. If no response has been received by December 15 of the funding year, the panel asks the group's church-member sponsor to obtain one.
3. The panel evaluates the previous year's grants in a report to the SRC, which will be passed along to the board.

Duties of Social Investment Fund Panel Members

1. Select a chairperson and clerk to keep minutes. Other panel members will be expected to help with writing notices for the newsletter, phoning, etc.
2. Publicize availability of money, guidelines, and application deadline in the newsletter and from the pulpit.
3. Set a date and times for presentations by applicants and notify applicants of their specific times.
4. Publicize this date and the names of groups that have applied in the church newsletter; invite the congregation to attend.
5. Read applications before the meeting and formulate questions.
6. Attend the Grants Panel meeting to choose groups to be funded.
7. Announce results: notify the board, and put a notice listing the panel's choices and a description of each in the newsletter.
8. Notify groups not chosen and those chosen in writing. Each letter to a funded group should be given to the controller along with a request-for-payment form signed by an authorized SRC officer and an evaluation form. (The controller mails the letter, check, and evaluation form together.)
9. In December, make sure groups receiving funding the previous year have all sent in reports on how the money was spent, and evaluate last year's funding.
10. Give a report to the SRC on what the panel did during the year and make recommendations for the future.

Sample 2

INSTRUCTIONS FOR OUTREACH GRANT APPLICANTS

Qualifications: Groups applying must be local nonprofit, nonpartisan, voluntary associations designed for community improvement and not already receiving direct aid from a committee or task force of the church or from another church fund. Proposals should be specific, measurable, achievable, and congruent with Unitarian Universalist values.

Deadline: Seven copies of the completed application and all attachments must be returned to the church office by the date specified on the application.

Sponsorship: Applications must be sponsored by a church member and signed by ten church-member supporters. Members may sign only one application. The sponsor must be familiar with the organization's operation and finances. All questions should be answered clearly and concisely; extra sheets or supporting information may be added if desired.

Presentations: A representative of each applicant organization will be asked to make a twenty-minute presentation to the Social Investment Grants Panel on the date agreed upon. (Specific appointments will be scheduled for each group.) Presentations should include a brief description of the organization and the project or activity for which funding is requested. Leave time for questions from panel members.

Funding Decision: The Grants Panel will evaluate the proposals and presentations in private and make recommendations to the congregation for approval of the grants at a congregational meeting (in March).

Grant Awards: Letters announcing grant awards and checks will be sent out on or before April 1.

Evaluations: Each organization that receives funding is asked to submit a report by December 1 to the Social Justice Outreach Grants Panel of the Unitarian Church, evaluating the project and describing how the money was spent.

For more information, contact _____ Chair of the Grants Panel at _____ (home) or _____ (work).

Sample 3

SOCIAL JUSTICE OUTREACH GRANT APPLICATION

1. Name, address, phone number of organization applying.

2. Name, address, phone number of organization contact person.

3. Name, address, phone number of person making presentation in person to the grants panel.

4. Has the organization received funding from the Social Justice Outreach Grants before?   If so, what year?

5. How should a check to the organization be made out?

   Address, if different from address above.

ORGANIZATION INFORMATION (Please be brief: Attach appropriate literature instead of filling out this form if the requested information is stated there.)

1. History of the organization

2. Statement of mission and goals

3. Description of current programs and activities

4. Number of paid staff   number of volunteers

5. Number of clients served

6. Current or projected annual operating budget   (please attach)

7. Current and projected sources of funding

8. Other organizations in the Rochester area serving the same or similar function

continues

Sample 3 *(continued)*

SPECIFIC REQUEST FOR SOCIAL JUSTICE OUTREACH GRANTS

1. Description of activities planned and items to be purchased

2. Timetable for implementation

3. Who and how many persons will be served

EVALUATION

1. Expected results from funding

2. How will you define and measure success?

3. A report back to the First Unitarian Church, Attn: Social Responsibility Committee, evaluating the project and describing how the money was spent is requested by December 1 of the funding year.

NAME, ADDRESS, AND PHONE NUMBER OF CHURCH-MEMBER SPONSOR

SIGNATURES OF CHURCH-MEMBER SUPPORTERS (ten)

1. _____   6. _____

2. _____   7. _____

3. _____   8. _____

4. _____   9. _____

5. _____   10. _____

Sample 4

THE COMMITTEES OF CORRESPONDENCE, 1772–2000:
A PROPOSAL

The Committees of Correspondence were created by the Boston town council in 1774 to protest the domination of the colonies by Great Britain. Samuel Adams, James Otis, Thomas Jefferson, Patrick Henry, and Richard Henry Lee were early members of a network that spread throughout the colonies and led to the successful Revolutionary War.

I propose a revival of these Committees of Correspondence to speak out on the dramatic changes brought on by the increasing political activity of the Religious Right, including the Christian Coalition, and other proposals from both sides of the political aisle.

While UUs may well differ on the nature of the revolution required, we can agree that the active participation of citizens is required. We cannot allow such drastic change without comment grounded in religious convictions. Our elected officials at all levels of government tell us that they are feeling the might of the Religious Right, but not the heft of the Religious Left (recognizing, of course, that while we are religiously left politically we are all over the map).

Each Sunday the Social Responsibility Council will be staffing a letter writing table focusing on different local, state, and national issues, with stamps, envelopes, paper, district maps, and background papers. We welcome your monetary contributions but we welcome your commitment to the just society even more.

Remember, we get the kind of government we deserve. Scary, isn't it?

Richard S. Gilbert

Sample 5

Petition: SOCIAL RESPONSIBILITY AGENDA ISSUE PPROPOSED FOR CONSIDERATION AT CONGREGATIONAL MEETING IN FALL

Issue

Definition of Social Problem

Religious Values That Apply

Goals and Objectives

Possible Strategies

PETITION (to be signed by voting members of the church; no one may sign more than one petition)

We believe that the social problem outlined above should be chosen as one of the priority issues for congegational focus during this church year.

I will work on the task force	I support the task force
1.	1.
2.	2.
3.	3.
4.	4.
5.	5.

Return to church office by

Church contact person   Phone

Sample 6

BOARD OF TRUSTEES GUIDELINES CONCERNING
SPECIAL CONGREGATIONAL MEETINGS DEALING
WITH CONTROVERSIAL ISSUES

I. A special congregational meeting dealing with a controversial social or political issue with serious ethical implications shall be called by the board of trustees pursuant to

  a. Presentation to the board of trustees of a petition signed by twenty-five or more church members.

  b. Action initiated by the board of trustees.

II. When such a special congregational meeting is called, the following procedure is recommended:

  a. That the board call an initial meeting for informational purposes only, allowing for the presentation of all sides of the issue in some suitable format, and

  b. That the board then call a special congregational meeting for the purpose of discussing and voting on the proposed action.

Sample 7

THE STRATEGIC PLANNING PROCESS: A HISTORICAL EXAMPLE

STEP ONE: DEFINITION OF THE PROBLEM TO BE ADDRESSED

The federal government plans to convert the athletes' housing area for the 1980 Winter Olympics into a youth prison following the games.

STEP TWO: STATEMENT OF ENVIRONMENTAL ASSUMPTIONS

(1) Lake Placid is an area remote from the cities from which the young prisoners would come. (2) Predominately white guards would supervise predominately black prisoners. (3) The United States ranks third highest in rate of incarceration in the world, behind South Africa and the Soviet Union. (4) The "Olympic Prison" will embarrass the United States in world opinion. (5) Prisons have a poor record of rehabilitation. (6) Alternatives to incarceration exist.

STEP THREE: STATEMENT OF RELIGIOUS ASSUMPTIONS

(1) We "covenant to affirm and promote the inherent worth of every person" (UUA bylaws). Therefore, each person is of worth, including prisoners. Prisons, by their very nature, tend to dehumanize people. (2) We also covenant to affirm and promote justice, equity and compassion in human relations. Prisons are unjust in that they incarcerate a disproportionate number of poor and minority people. (3) Affirming individual freedom, it is our task to maximize human choice consistent with social responsibility. (4) Human nature is not inherently bad but characterized by finite freedom. We must recognize human finitude in both offender, offended, and the community and seek to liberate that which is noblest in each. Alternatives to incarceration speak to this issue.

STEP FOUR: STATEMENT OF ACTION GOAL

To persuade the federal government to find more humanizing after uses for the facility (training site for athletes, public housing, etc.) and to begin implementing them by October 1980.

STEP FIVE: SELECTION OF A STRATEGY OR STRATEGIES

Strategy 1: To mount a massive public education campaign on the "Olympic Prison." Strategy 2: To call world attention to the "Olympic Prison" before, during, and after the 1980 Olympic Games. Strategy 3: To mobilize Unitarian Universalists and other citizen groups to put pressure on government officials to change the after-use plan.

continues

Sample 7 *(continued)*

STEP SIX: DEVELOPMENT AND IMPLEMENTATION OF TACTICS

Strategy 1 Tactics: (1) Launch a study group in the church to study the "Olympic Prison" in particular and the moratorium on prison construction in general within two months. (2) Persuade the minister (or guest speaker) to preach on the issue within the next month. (3) Develop a core of experts to begin a letter writing campaign over the next month, and make electronic media contacts within the next four months to obtain radio–TV exposure. Strategy 2 Tactics: (1) To place an ad in the *New York Times* and local newspapers at the time of the pregame competition. (2) To publicize the report of the UN Human Rights Subcommission on the prison immediately. (3) To demonstrate peacefully at the pregames and the Olympic Games themselves. Strategy 3 Tactics: (1) To maintain contact with the National Moratorium on Prison Construction Office. (2) To contact other prison action groups immediately. (3) To lobby Congress and launch a letter writing campaign to the president.

STEP SEVEN: EVALUATION OF THE PROJECT

The issue was effectively raised and placed on the public agenda. However, the facility became a prison following the games. What was learned? The power of the prison–industrial complex was (and is) immense. Perhaps this was an unrealistic goal. There are times of pyrrhic victories when, despite defeat, it was an important struggle to undertake. Social justice work often ends in temporary setbacks; winning is hardly guaranteed. Being faithful to one's principles is as important as succeeding.

Sample 8

STRATEGIC PLANNING PROCESS WORKSHEET

STEP ONE: DEFINITION OF THE PROBLEM TO BE ADDRESSED
(in one sentence)

STEP TWO: STATEMENT OF ENVIRONMENTAL ASSUMPTIONS

STEP THREE: STATEMENT OF RELIGIOUS ASSUMPTIONS

STEP FOUR: STATEMENT OF THE ACTION GOAL (specific, measurable, achievable, and consistent with the group's values)

STEP FIVE: SELECTION OF A STRATEGY OR STRATEGIES
Strategy 1:

Strategy 2:

Strategy 3:

STEP SIX: DEVELOPMENT AND IMPLEMENTATION OF TACTICS
Strategy 1 tactics:

Strategy 2 tactics:

Strategy 3 tactics:

STEP SEVEN: EVALUATION OF THE PROJECT (ongoing)
Changes made:

Group morale:

What has been learned?

Selected Bibliography

Adams, James Luther. *An Examined Faith: Social Context and Religious Commitment,* reprint ed. George K. Beach, ed. Boston: Beacon Press, 1991. More James Luther Adams essays.

———. *On Being Human Religiously: Selected Essays in Religion and Society,* 2nd ed. Max L. Stackhouse, ed. Boston: Skinner House Books, 1986. An excellent and challenging statement on social ethics by the late James Luther Adams, perhaps the foremost theologian and social activist in the Unitarian Universalist movement during the twentieth century.

———, and Seward Hiltner. *Pastoral Care in the Liberal Churches.* Nashville, Tenn.: Abingdon Press, 1970. A fine anthology focusing on the interrelationship of personal and social religion from a Unitarian Universalist perspective. See especially "Social Ethics and Pastoral Care" by James Luther Adams, pp. 174–220.

Alexander, Scott W., ed. *Salted with Fire: Unitarian Universalist Strategies for Sharing Faith and Growing Congregations.* Boston: Skinner House Books, 1994. See especially "Deeds Speak Louder" by John A. Buehrens, pages 159–167, and "Slaying Dragons of Hate with Ribbons of Love" by Marilyn Sewell, pp. 249–256.

Bellah, Robert Neelly, ed. *Habits of the Heart: Individualism and Commitment in American Life,* updated ed. Berkeley: University of California Press, 1996. A classic study of civil religion and American culture.

Boorstin, Daniel J. *The Lost World of Thomas Jefferson,* rev. ed. Chicago: University of Chicago Press, 1993. A fascinating look at the philosophy of Thomas Jefferson.

Buehrens, John A., ed. *The Unitarian Universalist Pocket Guide,* 3rd ed. Boston: Skinner House Books, 1999. See especially the chapter "Our Work for Social Justice and Diversity" by Jacqui James and Meg Riley, pp. 39–48.

——— and Church, Forrest, *A Chosen Faith.* Boston: Beacon Press, 1998. A discussion of the Principles of the Unitarian Universalist Association.

Carter, Stephen L. *The Culture of Disbelief: How American Law and Politics Trivialize Religious Devotion.* New York: Doubleday, 1994.

Church, F. Forrester. *God and Other Famous Liberals: Reclaiming Bible, Flag, and Family from the Far Right.* New York: Walker & Co., 1996.

Coles, Robert. *The Moral Life of Children.* New York: Atlantic Monthly Press, 2000.

Commager, H. S. *Theodore Parker: Yankee Crusader.* Magnolia, Mass.: Peter Smith, 1984.

Cousins, Norman. *In God We Trust: The Religious Beliefs of Our Founding Fathers.* New York: Harper & Row, 1958. An intriguing study of religion in the Revolutionary era, with special attention to John Adams and Thomas Jefferson.

Eisler, Riane. *The Chalice and the Blade: Our History, Our Future.* Magnolia, Mass.: Peter Smith, 1994.

Emerson, Ralph Waldo. *Nature Addresses and Lectures.* Temecula, Calif.: Reprint Services.

Foote, Henry Wilder. *The Religion of Thomas Jefferson.* Boston: Beacon Press, 1947. A revealing portrait of Jefferson's religion.

Frankl, Viktor. *Man's Search for Meaning: An Introduction to Logotherapy.* Boston: Beacon Press, 2000. The development of logotherapy out of the author's death camp experiences.

Freire, Paulo. *The Pedagogy of the Oppressed,* 2nd ed. New York: Continuum, 2000. A revolutionary understanding of the relationship between education and liberation.

Frost, Edward A., ed. *With Purpose and Principle: Essays about the Seven Principles of Unitarian Universalism.* Boston: Skinner House Books, 1998. See especially the author's essay "We Affirm and Promote Justice, Equity and Compassion in Human Relations," pages 31–44, and the essays "We Affirm and Promote the Goal of World Community with Peace, Liberty and Justice for All" by John Buehrens, pages 79–90, and "We Affirm and Promote Respect for the Interdependent Web of All Existence of Which We Are a Part," by Barbara Merritt, pages 91–101.

Gilbert, Richard S. *Building Your Own Theology,* 2nd ed. Unitarian Universalist Association, 2000. A study course designed to help Unitarian Universalists develop their own credos.

———. *Ethics: An Exploration in Personal Morality.* Unitarian Universalist Association, 1994. A study course designed to help participants create an ethical philosophy.

———. *How Much Do We Deserve? An Inquiry in Distributive Justice,* 2nd ed. Boston: Skinner House Books, 2001.

———. *In the Holy Quiet of This Hour.* Boston: Skinner House Books, 1995. A meditation manual published by the Unitarian Universalist Association.

Gilligan, Carol. *In a Different Voice: Psychological Theory and Women's Development,* reprint ed. Cambridge, Mass.: Harvard University Press, 1993. An important statement differentiating how women and men approach ethics differently.

Gurko, Miriam. *The Ladies of Seneca Falls: The Birth of the Woman's Rights Movement.* New York: Schocken Books, 1976. A historical analysis featuring Susan B. Anthony, among others.

Hamilton, Alexander, ed. *The Federalist Papers,* Denver, Colo.: Mentor, 1999.

Hammarskjold, Dag. *Markings,* reprint ed. New York: Ballantine, 1993. A brilliant collection of meditations by the late United Nations secretary general.

Harpers Bible Dictionary. New York: Harper & Brothers, 1959.

Holmes, John Haynes. *I Speak for Myself. The Autobiography of John Haynes Holmes.* New York: Harper & Brothers, 1959.

Hopkins, Charles H. *The Rise of the Social Gospel in American Protestantism, 1865–1915.* reprint ed. New York: AMS, 1967.

Houff, William H. *Infinity in Your Hand: A Guide for the Spiritually Curious,* 2nd ed. Boston: Skinner House Books, 1994. See especially the chapter "The Spiritual Basis for Social Action," pp. 169–77.

Jack, Homer A. *Denominational Social Action.* Chicago: Meadville/Lombard Theological School, 1944. A doctoral dissertation tracing Unitarian institutional social action up to World War II.

James, William. *The Varieties of Religious Experience: A Study in Human Nature,* reprint ed. Hampshire, UK: MacMillan, 1997. A classic analysis of religious experiences with a distinctly mystical orientation.

Jones, William R. *Is God a White Racist? A Preamble to Black Theology.* Boston: Beacon Press, 1998.

Mendelsohn, Jack. *Being Liberal in an Illiberal Age.* Boston: Skinner House Books, 1995.

———. *Channing, The Reluctant Radical.* Boston: Skinner House Books, 1979.

Merton, Thomas. *Conjectures of a Guilty Bystander,* reprint ed. Garden City, N.Y.: Image, 1968. Reflections on theology and culture by the late Trappist monk.

Mills, C. Wright. *The Causes of World War Three,* reprint ed. Armonk, N.Y.: M.E. Sharpe, 1985.

Morrison-Reed, Mark D. *Black Pioneers in a White Denomination,* 3rd ed. Boston: Beacon Press, 1994.

Muir, Fredric John. *A Reason for Hope: Liberation Theology Confronts a Liberal Faith.* Carmel, Calif.: Sunflower, 1994.

Niebuhr, Reinhold. *Moral Man and Immoral Society.* Magnolia, Mass.: Peter Smith, 1987. A classic statement of the bounds of human nature and their implications for social justice.

O'Hare, Padraic, ed. *Education for Peace and Justice.* San Francisco: Harper & Row, 1983.

Palmer, Parker J. *The Active Life: A Spirituality of Work, Creativity, and Caring.* San Francisco: Jossey-Bass, 1999. A personal testimony by a Quaker who uniquely combines spirituality and social action.

———. *A Company of Strangers: Christians and the Renewal of America's Public Life.* New York: Crossroad, 1985. Another in a series of books struggling with the issue of public–private dualism.

Parke, David B., ed. *The Epic of Unitarianism: Original Writings from the History of Liberal Religion.* Boston: Skinner House Press, 1985.

Parker, Theodore. *Theodore Parker's Experience as a Minister.* Boston: Rufus Leighbor, Jr., 1959. A moving statement by Parker addressed to his congregation as his health declined.

Phillips, Roy D. *Transforming Liberal Congregations for the New Millennium.* St. Paul, Minn.: Unity Church–Unitarian, 1996.

Rawls, John. *A Theory of Justice,* rev. ed. Cambridge, Mass.: Belknap, 1999. One of the most comprehensive statements of ethics in the twentieth century.

Robertson, D.B., ed. *Voluntary Associations: A Study of Groups in Free Societies.* Richmond, Va.: John Knox Press, 1966. These essays in honor of James Luther Adams provide a theoretical basis for church involvement in social problems.

Schweitzer, Albert. *Reverence for Life: An Anthology.* New York: Irvington, 1993.

Smith, Kenneth L., and Zepp, Ira G., Jr. *Search for the Beloved Community: The Thinking of Martin Luther King, Jr.,* reprint ed. Valley Forge, Pa.: Judson Press, 1998. A unique discussion of the theological, ethical, and social thought of the great civil rights leader.

Thandeka. *Learning to Be White: Money, Race, and God in America.* New York: Continuum, 2000. A controversial look at racism today from an African American theologian.

Unitarian Universalist Association Commission on Appraisal. *Interdependence: Renewing Congregational Polity.* Boston: Unitarian Universalist Association, 1997. A comprehensive study of the denomination with a chapter on social responsibility work.

———. *Unitarian Universalism and the Quest for Racial Justice.* Boston: Unitarian Universalist Association, 1993.

Voss, Carl Hermann. *A Summons unto Men: An Anthology of the Writings of John Haynes Holmes.* New York: Simon and Schuster, 1971.

Welch, Sharon D. *A Feminist Ethic of Risk,* rev. ed. Minneapolis, Minn.: Fortress Press, 2000. An articulate application of feminist theology to social justice.

Wilbur, Earl Morse. *A History of Unitarianism in Transylvania, England and America.* Boston: Beacon Press, 1964.

Wright, Conrad, ed. *A Stream of Light: A Short History of American Unitarianism,* 2nd ed. Boston: Skinner House Books, 1989.

Wuthnow, Robert. *Acts of Compassion,* reprint ed. Princeton, N.J.: Princeton University Press, 1993. A comprehensive discussion of religious motivation and social action.

Index

NOTES